WOODY ALLEN
Joking Aside

WOODY ALLEN
Joking Aside

Gerald McKnight

W.H. ALLEN · LONDON
A Howard & Wyndham Company
1982

Copyright © 1982 by Gerald McKnight

Typeset by Phoenix Photosetting, Chatham
Printed and bound in Great Britain by
Mackays of Chatham Ltd.
for the Publishers, W.H. Allen & Co. Ltd,
44 Hill Street, London W1X 8LB

ISBN 0 491 02767 2

Contents

Author's note

In case anyone is mystified by the chapter headings I have chosen, let me explain that they were inspired by the distinguished Jewish scholar Leo Rosten in his book *The Joys of Yiddish* (W.H. Allen, 1970). In his view, they reflect the influence of Jewish humour and philosophy on the English language. *Bubeleh* (say it as in 'boob-a-la') is a love-term for babies, and no doubt one of Woody's earliest pseudonyms. (Rosten tells of a Jewish boy's greeting by his mother after his first day at school: 'So, did you like school, bubeleh? You made new friends? You learned something, bubeleh? 'Yeah,' said the boy. 'I learned my name is Irving.')

I am also deeply grateful to the following: Tony Marshall, Virginia Field, Lee Guthrie, Roger Wood and staff of *New York Post*, Stephen Silverman, Guy Hortin, Peter Grimsditch, Anthea Disney, Jeffrey Blythe, Stan Mays, Joe Coggins, Kaye Webb, Joe Franklin, Abe Burrows, Max Liebman, Max Gordon, Art d'Lugoff, Moe Hack, Paula Cohen, Christopher Hewett, Fred Ebb, Mickey Rose, Bob Dishy, Estelle Parsons, Elaine Kaufman, Dr Dee Burton, Shirley Potter, Jack M. Roth, Linda Hersch, Prof. Jim Day, Dick Roffman, Mike Alber, Richard O'Brien, Nino Pantano, Tony Tamao, Barbara and Jerry Cohen, Barbara Loykovnova & David 11, Donald Newlove, Leonard Harrison (principal of Midwood High School), Pearl Roberts, Gladys Bernstein, Murray Eisenstadt, Morris Purcell, Margaret Bradshaw, Adrienne Adams, James Downing (principal of PS 99), C. 'Tex' Amdur, Gordon Willis, Ralph Rosenblum, Melvin Bourne, Randy Badger, David McGough, Ron Gallela, Roger Angell, Nancy Newlove, Ken McCormick, Nick Ludington, PEN Club, Players Club, Brooklyn Public

Library and Charles Richman. As always, I was greatly helped by my researcher, Paul Rossiter, my typist Merrilyn Cook, and more than I can say by those friends and colleagues who gave generous advice and assistance.

Gerald McKnight
Grimaud, France

April 1982

So why do you?

Woody Allen would have us believe that the only mystery about himself is why so many people find him mysterious. He tells us he never lies in interviews, because that way 'I don't have to remember what I said last time.' Now and again he exposes himself, if that is the word, to television and other interviews in various parts of the world; to lengthy chats with his friend Dick Cavett on New York's Public Broadcasting Services Channel 13. In England he has talked with seeming frankness and ease on British television. His books, films, plays, records and clarinet performances are public property as, he maintains, is so much of his life. Why then do we think of him as a delightful enigma?

The reason, quite simply, is that nobody – not even his family – can tell when Woody is putting it straight; when he is serious in what he constantly says about his early life (which we *know* was not as he makes his fictional characters appear to describe it); about his love affairs, passions, pleasures and pains. We are not told which of his utterances are, like his talented professional output, whimsical fancies of his puckish brain; and which are bare facts. We don't even know how autobiographical, if at all, any of his work is.

Is he having us on when he talks about sex? About God? Or about his need for analysis, and the complexes caused by his less than average height? There never has been a reliable way of knowing this; no guide to the genesis of the world's most sophisticated clown since Charlie Chaplin. We can only, he seems to be telling us, take him as we find him; or leave him alone. Preferably the later.

So the writer who edges close enough to look behind this mask is in for a tough time, as I found. First, Woody does not welcome having the levity dissected from the gravity of what he is on record of having said about himself and others. Secondly, he regards everything private and personal in his life – love affairs, marriages and so forth – as nobody's business but his own. Finally, he wields a remarkable power over many of those who know him intimately enough to lift the curtain. They refuse to say one word 'without his consent'. It is, in my experience, never forthcoming.

Yet, to appreciate what it is in Woody's work that makes xylophones of our funny-bones, there is an understandable wish to know more about Woody, the man. To strip the joker from the complex, neurotic, sometimes surreal nature of Woody's *oeuvre*; his curiously mixed bag of creative gems ranging from his passionately serious film *Interiors* to the hilarious slapstick of such early movies as *Take the Money and Run*, and leading to the sheer cine-magic of *Annie Hall* and *Manhattan*.

In his writings, also, one asks where the take-off point lies, divorcing the simple clowning of much of his early stage and film work from the satirical, cerebral wit of his *New Yorker* pieces?

What, in fact, is left once we rid Woody of his veils and see him without cap and bells, joking aside? The harder I looked, the more difficult it became to discern. When eventually I decided to attempt an answer in a book about him, it was out of admiration and curiosity combined; shared, I knew, by a multitude of his fans. But there was another reason. Woody, in refusing as he politely but firmly did, to let me interview him or to have his help in any way had put me on my mettle.

He did not deny my right to write a book about him, he said; but he did not welcome it on the following grounds: that a) there was little new to be said, b) that he might one day wish to write it himself and c) that he simply did not have time to spare for such a project. His words left me with the feeling a mountaineer must have on standing at the foot of the peak of peaks. Everest, after all, is no more 'there' than Woody Allen.

So was there no *other* way? No help available from those around him? Everything I heard was deeply depressing. Those who knew Woody or had worked with him warned: 'You won't get anywhere. He talks to nobody outside his own tight little circle. He is practically a recluse. His idea of a holiday is to lie on his bed in his New York apartment with the blinds drawn and the air conditioning on. He's afraid of elevators breaking down and hates wool next to his skin.'

Well, this was not quite so, fortunately. One close friend did talk to me about him, several times. So too did several of those who work in studios, theatres and publishing offices with him. I found people who not only shared my curiosity but who could and did materially assist in satisfying it. A chance meeting on a bus in Fifth Avenue, for instance, led to my discovery of Woody's parents in Florida and to my talking to his mother.

Not everything was easy, by any means. As I have said, everyone I approached who felt it necessary to ask Woody's permission to talk to me was it seems asked not to do so. His first wife telephoned me across the Atlantic to discuss a measure of collaboration which, somewhat mysteriously, was later withdrawn. My requests to the ladies in his life were universally rejected. There were those, like his manager Jack Rollins, who tried to qualify what they had said to me later.

However, the search for the real Woody Allen did not, as I discovered, depend solely on these. From the helpful teachers of his schools, from many old schoolmates, and from those who have known Woody at various stages and ages in showbusiness and in his ordinary existence, I learned much about him which, I believe, has never before been disclosed. How it explains the man behind the mask I must leave to those who read on.

All I can vouch for is that this biographical sketch, drawn as it necessarily was from remembered accounts and hearsay, is as accurate a definition of that maker of magic tales, in celluloid and print, Woody Allen, as I could make it. I shall be interested to know if, when he has read it, he still believes there is nothing new to be said.

Listen, bubeleh . . .

In 1952, when Alan Stewart Konigsberg entered his senior
year at Midwood High School in the Flatbush district of
Brooklyn, Morris Purcell's social studies class was where
the undersized were privileged to sit up in front, provided
they were attentive.

Alan's classmates called him 'Red' after his reddish hair.
As one of the shortest and smallest of his set (one section of
the 720 students in Midwood's massive Class of '53) he was
more privileged than most: allotted a seat in the first row of
desks. Closest to the dais from which Mr Purcell held forth.
It was only one place in from the door. And always, sitting
there, he could be seen to be studiously writing.

'Alan was so quiet that for a long time I believed he was
taking notes of what I was saying,' Mr Purcell recalls. 'Then
I heard that he was writing and telling gags to newspapers
and I got a look at what he was so busily writing. Sure
enough it was a list of gags which came into his head while I
was teaching.'

Morris Purcell taught history as well as social studies. In
1953 Midwood's class of Seniors were being put through
their last and final year's work before graduation. Without
the school's knowledge, or any tinge of personal shame,
young Konigsberg had already embarked on a career for
which no diploma would be necessary, or of value. Under
the pen name of Woody Allen, which his father believes
was coined from Alan's practise of carrying a baseball bat to
street games with friends (but which could equally have
derived from reflected adoration of Woody Herman among
the jazz musicians of the period) he was earning twenty-

13

five dollars a week writing gags in batches of fifty for a Manhattan agent, the late David Alber.

It is not easy to do this and pay attention to school lessons as well. The dual role took time and effort, as well as placing demands on him which he was far from ready to answer. Which way lay the light? His mother and father, more particularly Mrs Konigsberg, were constantly warning and worrying him. Theirs was the unshakable instinct for survival which only material success, the respectablity of sound education and solid achievement, could bring.

For Martin and Nettie Konigsberg, of European Jewish descent, there was no substitute for knowledge. No better passport to unassailable security than a Midwood diploma with high honours, followed by a college degree; thus leading to steady, gainful employment in banking, insurance, medicine, the law or one of the higher reaches of business, commerce and industry.

How could he argue? Faced with these heavily bourgeois pressures, Alan (Woody) did what he has since made an habitual practice of doing in any emergency. He kept mute and fled. Making a joke of it, he admits: 'I ate my meals in the cellar, or in my room; never with my family.' Indeed, he clung to his room like a hermit-crab to its shell, spending long hours locked inside among the pursuits and self-taught accomplishments of his own bent: magic, music and comic books. There Woody seems to have spent as much time mastering the sleight of hand and fingering of a B-flat Böhm system clarinet as absorbing calculus and the drier facts of American history. The exploits of Hair-Breadth Harry, High-Gear Homer and Tad of the Tanbark (as portrayed in *The Brooklyn Daily Eagle*) were in any case closer to his psyche than those of Christopher Columbus or Moses. He was an entrenched mollusc of a boy, whose passive resistance to parental and scholastic entreaties would have drawn admiration from Mahatma Ghandi. To the long-suffering Morris Purcell he was additionally irritating but for another reason entirely.

'Alan was always slow to get to his feet in class and answer my questions. He was not like any of the others. I'd

14

ask a question, then perhaps select a particular student to answer it in front of the whole class. Whenever it was Alan's turn, he'd stay seated for several seconds as if he hadn't even heard it, or did not have a thought about how to give a reply. He'd sit saying nothing at all. And we all had to wait.

'But then the astonishing thing was – as I well remember – he'd get up, *in his own time,* and give an answer that was *always* a hundred per cent right!'

In its way, this only made things worse. Came the day when Mr Purcell threw out a question to the whole class which had long been among his favourite standards when teaching Seniors approaching graduation. 'Given the opportunity,' he asked them, 'please describe for us what career you would most like to follow. And why.' .

It had never failed. A buzz of interest sirened through the class. Hands shot up. Alan, removed for some forgotten misdemeanour to the back of the class on this occasion, was one of the first to thrust out an anxious arm. Mr Purcell remembers, almost with glee:

'I kept him waiting. And all the time he was jumping up and down in his seat, waving his arms like a drunken windmill. Eventually, when there was hardly any more time before bell, I let him have the floor.'

Alan rose. 'I would like to be a sanitation worker,' he said.

There was a pause of disbelief, then a choke of suppressed laughter. The class erupted. 'But I had to be sure young Alan Konigsberg wasn't mocking me,' Mr Purcell says. 'I took a good, long look. In fact, he seemed perfectly serious. He wasn't joining in the laughter at all.

' "You mean you'd like to spend the rest of your life as a men's room attendant, or something like that?" I asked gravely. "Is that *really* the height of your ambition, Alan?"

'I was genuinely astonished. But Alan, for once, was ready with an answer. As soon as the class had quietened down he gave it, in his quiet, almost whiney voice.

' "You see, Mr Purcell", he said, "the way I see it is that a job as a sanitation worker would give me scope to do what I

15

really *want* to do. I'd earn money, and still have all the time I need to write and review plays and operas. Unless I get a regular job, like a men's room attendant, I'll never be able to do that and make enough to eat. Not at first anyway".'

The bell was about due. The class were getting out of hand, guffawing and twisting in their seats to see this funny little guy make his plea for a better world. Mr Purcell decided this flight of delirious fancy had to be checked.

' "Well, Alan," he said sharply. "I became a teacher because I wanted to stay clean. It seems you want to become a sanitation worker because you must like dirt." '

As he now says: 'It wasn't a very smart riposte, but he'd taken my breath away.'

The bell rang. Mr Purcell dismissed the class. He did not see Alan as he made his exit. He was surrounded by jeering classmates.

Nettie Konigsberg, born Nettea Cherrie, had married Woody's father when he and the whole Western world were struggling through the depths of the great depression following World War 1. Unemployment was cutting through American manhood like a scythe. It was fortunate that Martin 'Marty' Konigsberg could turn his hand to most things and did so, to keep a roof over his small family's head. But his trade, the only one in which he had acquired skill, was as an engraver of jewellery.

In more plentiful days there had been a comfortable living to be made from handwork of this sort. Any number of well-heeled customers were anxious to 'personalise' gifts and possessions. The depression had blown all that away.

With the early Thirties there was less and less work for an engraver's stylus. Machines were invented to do more cheaply and quickly what trained hands could do little better. Marty drifted from job to job, working for a while as a waiter in the renowned tourist tavern, Sammy's Bowery Follies, in lower Manhattan, just off Broadway. At Sammy's the waiters were required to sing, to give guests an impression of happy-go-lucky bonhomie in the German *biergarten* tradition, so he sang. But there was little song, or joy, in

Marty's heart.

While serving at table, or behind the long bar, he was constantly aware of the long, desolate lines of cheap-liquored 'bums' parading the notorious Bowery outside. Snoring, spitting and scratching their flea-bitten hides these desolate waifs set up bed-spaces along the sidewalks. To the customers their squalid wretchedness was merely a part of the colourful scene. But to the waiters this product of a city in the grip of the worst depression known to capitalist man was iced with dread.

To lose one's job might be to join the bums outside. How many engravers were among them, Marty had to ask himself? Woody's father worked as a cab driver during those penurious days. That was probably his lowest task. But sometimes, when his luck was in, he was remembered and favoured by some of his old professional associates. For quite some time Marty was employed at a jewellery store in the SoHo district of Manhattan, close to Chinatown. This shop, in Eldridge Street, appears mercifully to have disappeared, along with the bitter memory of those anxious days.

Woody's parents-to-be and many other young couples, in Brooklyn and elsewhere, found it hard to rid themselves of the fear and uncertainty of those years. For Marty, the news that Nettie was pregnant, brought to him in the spring of 1935, must have seemed like a ray of sunshine after a storm that had gone on far too long. Even then, it was still rumbling in the outer recesses of his existence.

As the time approached for Nettie's confinement there was comfort in prayer for those like Marty, brought up in the Jewish faith. And when on 1 December that year, a cold cloudy day in Brooklyn with light snow forecast and an overnight cold snap in prospect, he was told that Nettie had given birth to a son, his joy and relief were about evenly matched.

The house on Avenue K she brought him home to was no mean dwelling. But already the street – indeed the whole district – was changing. No. 1906 is remembered as a fine frame building, two storeys tall with lawn and shrubs stretching out toward the tree-lined pavement from a commodious porch. Today, it has given place to a gloomy hive of an apartment building covering the corner and extending back along Ocean Avenue.

The neighbours were Minnie Hollander, Henry Goodman, Jacob Nash and Ira Warm, soon to be replaced by Doris Wallach, Maude Solomon, Natalie Cohen, Esther Fieldberg and Irving Strong. They were there to smile and wave at Woody on his way to and from school. The problem for his father, as for many another in those difficult days, was to pay the rent and still put food in his family's belly and clothes on his son's back.

Between Woody's birth and graduation seventeen years later, this first home passed through a variety of hands. Speculation in property was thriving in Brooklyn. The Konigsbergs' prized corner site, where Woody treated the lawn with boyish indifference, was valuable land, ripe for development, part of a 'parcel' of neighbouring plots. Groups were formed, in which investors could secure as little as a sixteenth of a promising estate while waiting for the rest of the jigsaw to fall into place.

The Konigsbergs' rented house certainly changed ownership four times during Woody's time there, but he was probably unaware of these transactions. The impression his films create of Flatbush, indeed of Brooklyn, as a noisy, soulless area of decaying buildings and grasping paupers is extraordinary. In his day it was far more salubrious than it is today.

Five presidential elections came and went without any apparent help from his parents. The Konigsbergs' seeming lack of political interest was not, in a local historian's view, at all unusual. 'Perhaps half the residents of Flatbush failed to vote.' Either lack of concern, or understanding, was frequently the reason, though it could also have been due to lack of citizenship. Many who settled in Brooklyn were emigrants from Hitler's Europe, awaiting naturalisation. In some cases they were unable to speak English with any fluency.

Yet one need not imagine Woody's childhood as a ghetto

of poverty-stricken immigrants. Flatbush was far from being a mere Ellis Island halt for the flood of Russian, Polish, German and Scandinavian Jews seeking shelter in the accomodating USA. Those who were lucky enough to come to Brooklyn, and especially to the pleasant street where Woody lived, would have found a community of well-to-do residents with first-class schools and community facilities. Midwood district was officially described in 1957 as 'a section of upper middle income families . . . comprised of private homes, a few high rental apartment houses . . . the majority falling into that of expensive private accomodation.'

Very different from the Coney Island clangour of Woody' origins suggested skilfully in his work and which can so easily be taken as reflecting his own early involvement, despite his insistence that his films and stories are 'not autobiographical'.

I should have such luck

Under the veneer of middle-class respectability, Flatbush too was having its problems, especially with the young. In the year Woody left his junior school, Public School 99, a Special Session Justice, Myles A. Paige, warned parents at a meeting of the Greater Flatbush Civic League that 'they're not supervising children as they should'. Justice Paige pointed to rising numbers of youthful crimes, muggings and gangfights in the neighbourhood. 'In the majority of cases,' he told a Chamber of Commerce audience, 'there is a background of drug addiction.'

Woody would have had to be blind, deaf and dumb not to know that some of his classmates were among those who at least sampled drugs. His own belief that all drugs are dead-end routes to nowhere was no doubt born out of those early, often tragic, situations. The school grapevine buzzed with dramatic tales of students caught in drug and crime webs. They certainly seem to have given Woody a lasting signpost to where the primrose path led.

From his earliest days at PS 99 on East 10th Street (a slightly longer walk from his home than Midwood), Woody was always anxious to avoid trouble. In appearance he was remarkably well turned out. How much this was due to his mother's care, Nettie Konigsberg is not prepared to admit, but it is worth considering. The photograph of him taken with his final PS 99 class shows a remarkable contrast to the man he has become.

'He'd have worn a clean white shirt and green tie in those days,' the present principal of PS 99, James Downing, asserts. Mr Downing has been the school's headmaster for the past nine years. 'If Woody dresses casually on formal occasions now,' (such as when he affects sneakers or gym-shoes with evening dress) 'it could be a reaction to those days,' another teacher says.

Weekly Assembly of Woody's form in the elementary school's main hall was an occasion when every student was expected to be especially tidy and well-groomed. PS 99 was then some 1600 strong (reduced today to less than 700). In those days of Flatbush prosperity, boys and girls who went there were taken through to eighth grade, with no need to go on to Junior High School (if that was their destiny, as in Woody's case it was) before going to Midwood. Graduation from both was a matter of considerable local pride.

The really strange thing was the way Woody seems to have melted into the middle distance, as if afraid of too close a contact with the rougher elements of the world around him. 'Woody didn't work well in school,' muses an old schoolfriend, 'on the other hand, he was a remarkably good self-study. A self-taught genius, I'd say.'

But the teachers he had at PS 99, where he went in the year after the war ended, 1946, are still trying to convince themselves that Woody was there at all. They have his record sheet. And that school photograph, taken in his final year (1949) when he was eleven and in eighth grade. But recalling anything about one of their most triumphantly successful pupils has been frustrating for them, to say the least.

Old Mrs Eudora Fletcher, who was principal in Woody's days at the school, is dead. She ran PS 99 with a stern belief in the stick and carrot theory: plenty of stick for the wrong-doers, an occasional carrot for the triers. Which of these Woody belonged to is largely forgotten, though he appears never to have been in any serious trouble there.

'Tex' Amdur was the assistant principal. He says he would certainly have know if Woody had been in any hot water. 'I don't recall him at all,' he says. 'And I would have, because I was the "bad man". When they were naughty, they were sent to me. I'll tell you, it was a tough school in those days. And if Woody, Alan Konigsberg, had been told to see me for any serious misdemeanour I'd remember it, very clearly. So would he!'

Another of Woody's PS 99 teachers, Lilian Rosenberg strives vainly to think back to when he was just one of the bright young faces in those old classrooms with the ornate brass doorhandles and worm-eaten desks. 'I honestly can't remember him among my students,' she says. 'There was a Konigsberg in my class (which was for the really bright ones, in social studies and other subjects). But it wasn't Woody, I'm almost sure. Of course, I'm over eighty now and it was a long time ago. But I've discussed it with other teachers, and *none* of us can call him to mind.'

According to 'Tex' Amdur the only one who did remember him, to his knowledge anyway, was Theresa Reilly, Woody's PS 99 history teacher. 'She too is dead now,' he says. 'But she knew him all right. It was how he made out in her class that she wasn't too sure about.' He shakes his head. 'I'd say Woody just wasn't outstanding when he was here. That's about all you can say.'

PS 99 students in those days were nearly all white. And Mrs Fletcher had made the school into one of the best scholastic-average academies in the City of New York. It was, in fact, one of the prize schools in the whole USA – unique in some ways, because of the potential it offered its students to stay on right through to High School. (Most elementary public schools still send their alumni on to Junior High School for two years before High School.)

So Woody, because he only came there in fifth grade – either because he'd just come to the district, or because he'd been at Hebrew School before that – faced stiff competition.

This may well have been where his early accounts of being bullied by bigger boys were enacted in real life. His small build (though he claims he was a success at boxing), his red hair, and his pronounced shortness of vertical inches may all have acted as goads to any brute of a boy who enjoyed terrorising younger and punier schoolmates. 'We can never tell what goes on *after* school,' 'Tex' Amdur says complacently. Not even Eudora Fletcher could do that, for all her Edwardian severity.

The point is that Midwood had to pick up where PS 99 left off with his development. If scars were left on Woody's psyche as a result of oppression from the physically dominant, they would have been particularly sensitive to Midwood's even more 'pushy' atmosphere.

Woody was twelve when he first entered High School in 1949. Arthur Miller, that other Brooklyn ingrate, was presenting his *Death of a Salesman* in faraway Broadway without Woody being more than casually aware of it, or him. None of the year's great films (Asquith's *The Winslow Boy*, Carol Reed's *The Third Man*, Melville's *Les Enfants Terribles*) are likely to have come his way. For Woody, the only important consideration was that it was his first year at Midwood.

In the main hall on entering the neo-classical, grey stone building on Bedford Avenue, having climbed the steps under the Romanesque portico supported by six towering columns, he was greeted by a formidable injunction. On the wall to his left was a plaque. Its message read: ENTER TO GROW IN BODY, MIND AND SPIRIT. DEPART TO SERVE BETTER YOUR GOD, YOUR COUNTRY, AND YOUR FELLOW MAN.

These were words which should have inspired both deeds and development in the young boy climbing those steps after walking the half-mile from the corner of Avenue K and Ocean. Sadly, Woody's growth was destined to occur outside rather than inside the school, and hardly at all in body. The school seems to have been little more than a straightjacket from which he could barely wait to be released.

At home, he no doubt had his own room when not forced by circumstances, and visiting relatives, to share with his baby sister. And it is interesting to compare this fact with the setting given to Woody's sad young hero, Steve, in his most recent Broadway play *The Floating Light Bulb*. Woody's would have been a room with a door which could and often was, one gathers, shut tight against any intruder. Steve's was merely an annex in which he was permanently made conscious of his family's violent disruption. The illusion that Woody was forced to endure a similar discordance is constantly fostered by his work, while being vehemently denied by him in real life.

Yet his shyness does raise the question: why, if his childhood and home life were no more wretched than that of any normal child, did he choose such solitary paths? Look again at *The Floating Light Bulb*. A Jewish couple are beset by poverty and the shiftiness of the father. As a consequence, the elder son (a boy of roughly Woody's age during his later schooling) has been reduced to stammering, self-conscious awkwardness. To escape, he practises magic. So too did Woody Allen.

While on a holiday (which he described to a friend as unutterably boring) he had discovered an interest in, and acquired some competence in, simple conjuring tricks. At school, the *Midwood Argus* newspaper warned that there was 'a motto among Red's (Woody's) friends which throws light on some of his magician's digital dexterity. "Never play cards with Konigsberg!"' He has claimed skill in sleight of hand ever since.

Woody's likeness to Steve, as in his tongue-tied shyness, is probably no more autobiographically accurate than, say, the Coney Island setting of the scene depicting the home background of Alvy Singer, the character he played so convincingly in his film *Annie Hall*. That was a parody of Brooklyn, certainly of Flatbush, suggesting a horror of rattling, overhead rails and dreary slums. If the film was largely self-inspired it also owed a lot to his imagination. Thus one learns to beware of judging Woody by the imagery of his pen.

In fact it is far more likely that boredom, and a marked distaste for the disciplines of threadbare respectability, drove him into the seclusion of his locked bedroom. These, and the withdrawal he instinctively made from over-zealous companionship were largely responsible. Around him was a chorus of persuasion to walk the conventional path towards academic success and achievement. From his neighbourhood rabbi to the pressing uncles and aunts who lent their weight to his parents' urgings, he was beset by good intentions. It may well explain why he found relief in something of a hermit's role whenever possible.

In addition, there was a lack of contact with kids his own age. Woody seems to have had few acquaintances, let alone friends. Gregariousness was never in his nature, and the need to talk at length to anyone on any subject which did not wholly interest him – Dixieland, basketball and the availability, or otherwise, of any pretty girl student who had caught his eye – may well have been almost as painful to him as having a tooth drilled.

It was not until he was in Junior year at Midwood that he made his first really important friend. Mickey Rose was a youth like himself, though six months older. He liked the same things. In some ways he was also the exact reverse. Woody despised Midwood: Mickey was delighted with it. He had longed, he says, to be sent to it in place of another school, Erasmus, which was closer to where he lived. 'I had a fantasy about Midwood being so much better. Surrounded by green grass and trees and open space.'

Friendship with Rose therefore was one of opposites. Yet they shared a great deal. 'We both loved to play baseball,' Mickey Rose remembers. 'We didn't play on any of the Midwood teams. But Woody and I were together on the same Police Athletics team, and that was a lot of fun for us both.'

Did Woody choose the Police team, or did they choose him as a form of community service? Though Rose says he cannot recall Woody being in bad odour with the law, their association dates only from Woody's penultimate year at Midwood, when they met in an Art Studies class. And unless Woody's tongue was in his cheek when discussing early misdemeanours with Larry Merchant of the *New York Post* it certainly seems that he had attracted police attention more than once.

According to Merchant (who certainly must have believed Woody was telling the truth) he had had three encounters with the law. First, when caught red-handed breaking into school to play ball. Hardly a major crime. But then there was the distinctly un-humorous accident when

25

he hit a lady with a pellet from his BB gun. And, later still, when a small fire he started got out of control.

These skirmishes on the frontiers of crime were no doubt in Woody's mind when he later maintained (as he jokingly did to early interviewers) that he would far sooner have become a criminal than imprison himself for life behind an office desk, or store counter.

Rose and he shared a number of adolescent interests. Girls and gigs, mostly. Other companions were less fortunate; Jack Budnitsky, for example, appears to have come close to Woody without ever gaining that friendship which others have found so durable. According to Woody's classmate at Midwood (and PS 99) Barbara Lieberman, who married another classmate Jerry Cohen, he and Woody often walked to school together. 'They were very close in the early days,' she maintains. 'Jack was probably the only friend Woody had then, I'd say. Nobody else bothered with him.' But Mrs Cohen admits, 'I myself didn't really notice him. To me, he was just another neighbourhood boy at my school.'

To Mickey Rose, on the other hand, Woody was an inspiring, amusing companion whose company enriched the times they spent together. Unlike Woody's more ambitious and conventional schoolfellows Rose was a young man who saw the funny side of life. He rejoiced in Woody's quirky humour, and they shared an almost identical belief that the world did not merit being taken too seriously.

It would seem that the notion that one day they should write something together sprang from this delight in the comic idiocy of so much in life. Many years later, when they decided to attempt the screenplay of a film in collaboration, they found – according to Rose – that they shared a common satirical viewpoint. It paid off handsomely, as the success of what became Woody's first self-directed film, showed.

Also, they were equally devoted to Dixieland jazz music, while most of their contemporaries were following the cult sounds and beat of rock and roll. 'This was something we both felt deep down, a real love of the early New Orleans rhythms,' Rose explains. 'Woody was determined to master his clarinet, forever playing and practising. And I was as crazy about it as he was.'

At his home in California which Woody visits whenever he is on the west coast, and where he stays with the Roses and their two children who know him as 'uncle Woody', Mickey still hankers after those carefree days. I played drums to express the best of that great stuff,' he says, 'and it's still something I absolutely love. In fact, I've got my drums packed away somewhere.'

Without too much persuasion, if his old friend should ask, there is little doubt Mickey Rose would be delighted to sit in with him again for another foot-stomping session of early jazz. Since he and Woody last worked together, on Woody's film *Bananas,* released in 1971, Rose has been writing and directing his own pictures. 'But whenever Woody comes out here and stays with us at the house,' he says, 'I'm tempted to drag those drums out of the cupboard again.'

The more and harder you practise music, the better your performance becomes. With girls it was often the opposite in Woody's case. The Midwood girls were an unfeeling lot. Those co-eds could be devastatingly cruel to a small fellow with no strong, outgoing personality or heroic football-team *macho* to attract their affections.

It was shameful, but Woody seems barely to have existed for the school's 'in' crowd of attractive young girls. As Barbara's husband Jerry Cohen recalls: 'He was a loner, always a loner. We used to hang out at *Cookies* on Avenue J with some of the prettier girls. It was a soda fountain used almost exclusively by us Seniors. But I don't remember Woody ever being one of the gang. He was pretty much a nonentity at the time, I'd say.'

Barbara his wife, who was in the same class with both of them, summed up Woody's failure to win the hearts and favours of the Midwood girls: 'There was terrific competition between us for the guys who really mattered. Woody was definitely not one of them. There were men whose buttons and hats were in great demand, because a girl who got given one was known to be dating the guy. Naturally, if he was a real catch, she then became the envy of all the other girls, and it was pretty important. I remember Woody slightly, but he didn't stand out in any way. And I certainly don't think any girl I knew craved his button or hat.'

Barbara was one of Midwood's most active students. She took part in student government and the annual choral concert put on by the school group know as 'Sing'. As she says, 'We wrote all our own lyrics, but Woody didn't do a thing for us as far as I know. If he did, it must have been in my absence because I never saw him take a hand in any part of it.'

Even the Seniors' Concert, *Vandal*, scheduled in the *Argus* to be performed that summer of 1953 (and for which they reported Woody had written a sketch: 'One of the writers of the June '53 Senior Show') never happened, she says. Some problem over examinations and who would, or would not be, available. Or did all those 'duties' the paper's reporter questioned Woody about stand in the way for some of the others, if not for him?

'Alan is well aware of his duties and responsibilities as a Senior,' the paper reported. 'He bears them with a sense of pride. In fact, says Alan, "I'd rather pay my Senior dues than eat – and that's the way it's gonna be for the next four months!" '

Though his gags were earning money, this suggests that Woody was short of cash. The reason was probably his diversity of interests: finding the subway fare to and from David Alber's Manhattan office weekly; buying the latest conjuring tricks; and providing himself with reeds and records, perhaps also sheet music (though there is no record of his having taught himself to read music). Then there were equally pressing demands on his purse from the world of entertainment. Woody, from an early age, devoured the films shown at the local cinema. He also formed a close and loyal attachment to the New York Giants and paid to see the baseball at nearby Ebbets Field whenever possible.

Lack of money could also have held back his growing quest for dates with girls. Mickey Rose remembers how hard Woody tried and how little he succeeded with the Midwood young ladies he invited out. Having Rose's companionship in these encounters may also have hampered him: the fact that his friend was eight inches taller accentuated his own shortness. Yet he persisted.

'Woody had a constant eye out for a pretty girl,' Rose recalls. 'We both did. But I don't think he scored while we were in school, certainly not as much as he would have liked. I'd say he based a lot of his film characters – the loser who triumphs in the end with girls like Diane Keaton – on the wish he must have had then that he could be more successful.'

Mickey Rose remembers Woody as 'always casually dressed' while Barbara Cohen disagrees: 'No, he was always *neatly* dressed. At Midwood, you had to be or you were sent home.' She remembers, 'We never got to be friendly, but that was because we weren't in the same section. I only sometimes saw him on the street. We both walked the same way to school so I must have passed him dozens of times. But the truth is,' she explains, 'Woody just didn't stand out for me. And afterwards, I went on to Brooklyn College and graduated there, by which time I'd completely lost touch with him.'

Losing touch with Woody has never been difficult. It is getting into touch, and holding his interest, which has been a hurdle for many of those who have come in contact with him. 'There was an awful lot he didn't like at school,' Mickey reminisces. 'Shakespeare, for instance. I remember he couldn't stand him; or maybe he didn't understand him, then. I know he hated having to learn the plays.'

It does seem that there was a deeply-rooted unhappiness lying at the heart of Woody's life during those early years in Flatbush. An unease of mind and senses so acute that nothing could cure it, but escape. He was small (a physical minority). Funny (an intellectual minority). And Jewish (an ethnic minority – though PS 99 and Midwood High School students were 'predominantly Jewish', according to James

Downing).

And Woody in his early development had ample reason to suspect that the world was no bed of roses for a boy from Brooklyn.

You should live so long

Described once by his friend Dick Cavett as 'raconteur, swordsman and breaker of hearts,' Woody Allen, in those early days, came close to being the opposite of all these things. He seems to have been slow to express himself, an undistinguished sportsman and far from successful with the opposite sex. His dislike of school may well have owed much to these handicaps. It also said something for the perception of Morris Purcell, Midwood history and social studies teacher who prompted Woody's 'sanitation-worker' admission, that he detected nobler qualities in him.

Purcell, more than most, sensed the extreme shyness which so often·glued Woody's tongue to the roof of his mouth, and which was to cocoon his inner life for many future years. He was one of the very few in the school faculty who noticed a curious blend of humanity and humour in the undersized student. As he clearly remembers, the day came when he had personal experience of both these qualities to an extraordinary degree.

'Woody,' Mr Purcell recalls, 'was fidgetting. I could see he was unusually concerned about something.' The boy was shifting about in his customary seat, close to the door in the front row of the class. It seemed he wanted to attract attention. 'But he didn't raise his arm for some time. I got the impression he didn't want to interrupt what I was saying to the class.'

When this had gone on for a while Mr Purcell turned to Woody with a questioning look, thinking that if he had anything to say he'd come out with it. But not Woody. He slid out of his seat, half raising his hand as if asking permis-

31

sion to leave the class, but instead he came up to where the teacher was standing and tried to whisper in his ear.

'Being so short, I couldn't get what he was saying at all,' Mr Purcell remembers. 'I had to bend down so that I could hear whatever it was he had to say, so privately. Only then did I learn what had been bothering him.

'"Mr Purcell, your fly is open," he whispered. I looked down and sure enough it was. I'd been forgetful about dressing myself properly that morning; with the result that a wide, irregular rectangle of shirt was gaping at the class. Young Alan could have made a song and dance about it, and no doubt the whole class would have enjoyed laughing at my discomfort. Instead, he'd chosen this way to try to help me get out of trouble.'

What surprised Mr Purcell when he thought about it afterwards was that Woody had seemed more embarrassed than he was. With great presence of mind the teacher immediately commanded the class to open their books at a page which he chose at random. While they searched and rustled, he diplomatically adjusted the error.

'I retired swiftly to the very back of the classroom to do it,' he says. 'After that, Woody seemed considerably less irritating to me.'

Morris Purcell had sensed in young Konigsberg a strain of concern rarely shown by students of his age. But this did not save the boy from bouts of humiliating anguish in clashes with authority.

Tony Tamao knew Woody at Midwood as the others did, as 'Red', the nickname earned by his thick crop of wavy auburn hair rising from a distinctive widow's peak. He has a vivid recollection of Woody in trouble. 'Red wasn't a friend of mine, being a year ahead in school, but I knew him by sight,' Tony explains. And I once saw him and another student being given a really hard time by a proctor.

'I happened to be passing and was therefore forced to witness the whole affair. The proctor had dragged them both out into the corridor in front of me. Woody was red in the face, red all over. I never did learn what had happened or what it was all about. But he sure seemed to be in plenty of trouble.'

Midwood, like every other major United States High School, produces a Year Book commemorating each class's graduation. In Woody's 'Epilog' all 720 of his 'Class of '53' are recorded with photographs, except a dozen or so 'camera shy' students (surprisingly, in view of his future dislike of being photographed, he was not among these) and details of scholastic and extra-curricular accomplishments. Under Alan Konigsberg (mis-spelt – deliberately? – 'Konisberg') there is nothing. Only blank space.

Since nobody from the school now remembers what the trouble could have been that Tony Tamao witnessed, this may explain it. 'A serious infringement of the rules, such as gross insubordination, stealing or cheating, could certainly result in erasure of all such credits,' one of the disciplinary staff explains today. There is no record of Woody having incurred any such penalty, nor do his teachers recall him having done so. Yet with the complete absence of any of those sought-after credits in the souvenir graduation issue of his class (and for a student who, in the present headmaster's view was above average), it remains a curious mystery. Did Woody's hatred of school originate with this lack of appreciation, or vice-versa? And can such a creative and talented youth have taken *no part at all* in the great parade of extra-curricular activities offered? 'It could be, but seems unlikely,' Murray Eisenstadt, another of his teachers (a great tennis enthusiast, and sometime Midwood's Dean of Boys) reflects. 'I know he was not, put euphemistically, one of the top students. And I know he was not in the photograph of our tennis team, which won the championship for the first time that year. Surprising, because I believe he is very fond of tennis. But I do know he was very quick to learn.'

As proof, Mr Eisenstadt declares: 'I had a friend, now dead, who took over his class in geometry. Max Weiss was a brilliant teacher. Woody had come up with only a sixty-five the previous year in the subject. Yet when Max coached him he got a ninety-two mark.'

Alas, other contemporary Midwood teachers' memories

run on less flattering lines. Jimmy Walker, one of Midwood's current maths teachers, was curious enough to ask Woody's English teacher, Joe Grubanier, before he died, how he did in his subject. He was told: 'His English was not good.' While it would be heartening to say of the writer who has since published three books (of his own writings in the *New Yorker* and other selective publications) that his marks argue otherwise, they do not. Woody's class mark for English was seventy-five, but in the all-important Regents Examination he is said to have scored only sixty-five.

To Gladys Bernstein, who taught special studies in his day, he was wasteful of all that Midwood offered. 'Woody's a genius,' she scoffs, 'but he's off the wall! He wants to blame the school for everything! Like playwright Arthur Miller who says the same things about his Abraham Lincoln High School in Brooklyn. They both hate their schools.'

She adds with feeling: 'This is a marvellous school. And in Woody's day it was even better. He didn't *do anything* here. He just went through the motions, getting sixty-fives in everything.'

When Mrs Bernstein's daughter, who is now a doctor in Manhattan, was a student at Barnard College she went to see Woody in his play *Play it Again Sam* on Broadway. Afterwards, she called backstage to meet him. She told Woody: 'I'm from Midwood High School.' She says he put his head in his hands to block his ears. 'Don't talk to me about it,' he said. 'I don't want to hear about Midwood. I *hate* that school!'

Not unnaturally, many Midwood staffers are proud of their school's connection with the now world-acclaimed Woody Allen. But Gladys Bernstein's view is shared by several of them. Knowledge that the school failed to do more than partially educate one of its most successful students bears hard on the faculty.

'I've heard he did a lot of crazy things when he was here,' Mrs Bernstein says. 'Don't ask me to go into details; we don't want to get involved with Woody Allen. He can blame the school, but it wasn't the school at all. It was the fact that he wouldn't do his lessons.'

A teacher who qualified with Woody in June '53, and has been at Midwood teaching social studies for thirteen years – Eugene Krinsky – says he feels piqued that Woody's later films have projected a rough and tough, Coney Island-style image of the Brooklyn he grew up in. 'This is completely false,' Mr Krinsky insists (with nodded approval from colleagues who remember Flatbush, and the Midwood sections of Brooklyn, in the Forties and Fifties). 'It was then a high middle-class, affluent neighbourhood. It has now gone down a lot, but it is still a good class area today. And when Woody was here at school, believe me you were *somebody* if you went to Midwood!' It was known then as a 'silk-stocking school'.

Another of Woody's long-suffering Midwood faculty, Mrs Margaret Bradshaw, says she barely remembers him. 'When you're handling over a thousand children, you can't remember them all,' she explains. 'And Woody, to me, was a nonentity.'

Mrs Bradshaw taught two special French classes for top stream students in which, she says, Woody was not represented. 'His average mark was only sixty-seven,' she says. 'Speaks for itself. He never had a demerit, or was in any sort of trouble here so far as I know. But he was bored and discontented – which, when you think of what the school had, and still has, to offer is incredible.'

The astonishing thing is that, in spite of all this, Woody *did* graduate.

In May 1952, when Woody was sixteen-and-a-half and in his final, senior year at Midwood High School (and already a budding professional gag writer, Flatbush celebrated its first, proud 300 years of existence.

What the *Brooklyn Eagle* described as 'the mellow bell' of Flatbush Dutch Reformed Church pealed out every night in the third week of the month to remind Woody, and the rest of the populace, of the historic founding. Articles were printed, speeches and lectures made and given, about the early Dutch settlers and English traders who had set up one of the country's largest slave-trading centres right there in Flatbush.

Woody's private thoughts may well have been more concerned with his own 'slavery' to Dr Ross (the then headmaster), Mr Purcell, and others among the Midwood faculty trying, with little success, to hammer education into him.

In less than a year's time he would, with any luck, be graduating, and with a professional career (though not the one his parents wished for him) already assured. How he managed so much in so little time may have had much to do with the inherited determination and energy of his father, but it also came as a reward for the long hours of solitude spent in his room after school.

Not only did he learn there an extraordinary degree of concentration (not least by the constant, continuous practice which mastery of magic tricks required) but his devotion to music was equally character-forming. He has often described how slavishly he worked at the difficult passages, no doubt seeking the same easy-sounding sweetness of tone and agility of fingering as the leading instrumentalists of his time. Records of these jazz masters, recorded at 78 rpm, were on sale locally – another pull on his slender pocket. There must have been other occasions when, either in Brooklyn or Manhattan, he could see and hear them in the flesh.

But it is mainly films he has since praised for opening his eyes to the outside world. And it was his own innate sense of parody and satire that distorted this vision for him. He was also developing an increasing appetite for reading books. At a certain time in his development it seems he abruptly turned from the trashier novels and magazines to devouring works of weight. If they coloured his imagination during his latter schooldays they did nothing to alter his lack of enthusiasm for the work Midwood set him to do.

Perhaps no school could have held sway against the persuasive flush of success which Woody had earned for himself with his gags. His work was not only being paid for, it was earning the respect of professionals like Alber. David Alber's acceptance of the first sheaf of 'one liners' from Woody's pen had been a remarkable achievement in one so young.

When the *Midwood Argus* reported, as it later did, how Woody owed his start as a writer to a relative in showbusiness ('who had heard his jokes and asked him to write some down'), this belittled his effort. As far as Alber's son Mike Alber knows, there was no relationship between Woody and his late father.

What seems to have attracted Alber was the unique quality of Woody's humour which expressed itself in wry, oblique comment on even the most serious subject. As agent for a number of celebrity showbusiness performers who hired him to keep their names constantly in the public gaze, Alber's first concern was publicity. 'Comprehensive press coverage is of immense importance,' he once wrote. 'Let the experts talk about "counsel". I think what's important is to cut the capers and get into the papers!'

By using writers like Woody, whose throwaway lines would appeal to newspaper columnists, and by tying these 'gags' to his clients, Alber created a cunning publicity technique. He became a vehicle for the continuous 'showcasing' of stars like Bob Hope who used his services. 'My father first spotted Woody' name in Earl Wilson's column,' Mike Alber remembers. 'He called to ask who he was, and Earl put them in touch. It astonished him to find that he was dealing with a young man still at school!'

In David Alber's career, astonishment seldom interrupted a good business deal. He promptly hired the schoolboy to write for him, demanding fifty gags a week as a regular delivery. 'Afterwards,' Mike Alber remembers, 'Woody used to come up to the office with his schoolbooks. He never failed to bring in his weekly quota of jokes, scribbled usually on two sheets of school paper.'

Both Mike and his father wrote gags themselves and were keen judges of humour. Mike Alber says that they both recognised and appreciated Woody's rare talent. It was, in fact, Mike who took over from Woody on his departure (and, as a matter of historic record, it was a young man called Mickey Rose who went to work for Alber later on, in the same capacity).

The Alber factory was feeding at least a dozen columnists in those days, all hungry for any line which would raise a chuckle or lift an eyebrow, and which they could (or Alber could) tie a big name to. The real writer was seldom mentioned, which made it thankless work. Woody soon came to realise that Alber's exploitation, helpful though it was, could only be a stepping stone. He probably also saw that what he could do so facilely for Alber – i.e. make people laugh with his pen and his native, near-black sense of comedy – could just as well be done for himself. The raw talent was there, as natural as sleep.

The trick was to achieve a dancing, quirky conflict between sense and nonsense. The material was a recorded impression of the absurdities of everyday life, a continuous parody of ineptitude. Farce somehow became credible. The themes of death, sex and human failings caught people off-guard, as if surprised in their underwear. They laughed because they recognised their more embarrassing and irreverent thoughts, if not actions, in Woody's words. His jokes poked wicked fun at a herd of sacred and conventional cows. By twisting normal events and relationships, as well as fears, he made people see themselves as faintly idiotic, though always it was 'the other guy' they laughed at – the man ahead of them on the street who slipped on the banana skin.

It is doubtful that Woody ever laughed at his own jokes. But once he had recognised that his was a most powerful and valuable weapon, one which could detonate charges strong enough to release all inhibition in an audience (and for which they would pay a high price), he came to his senses remarkably quickly. After all, with such a talent why should he waste his substance on press agency puffs? Why not go it alone?

My son the physicist

But Woody was still a schoolboy, and under pressure from his parents to go on to college. If he was to reach a wider market with his writing he would need help. Preferably it should come from somebody established in showbusiness, somebody whose recommendation would sow confidence. And such a man, by sheer good fortune, was at hand: Abe Burrows, one of Broadway's most celebrated showmen still today, whose credits include such hits as *Solid Gold Cadillac, Can-Can, Guys and Dolls* and *How To Succeed in Business Without Really Trying,* Burrows was a relative of the Konigsbergs, if only by marriage.

In Woody's budding career it was a momentous day when, no doubt with an appointment arranged on his behalf, he went to see the great man in his New York apartment. Burrows remembers it well. He had the impression that Woody was shy and apprehensive, a tongue-tied teenager in his final High School year, outwardly giving no hint of any great dynamism or professional zeal.

It was only after Burrows had let Woody in and sat him down that Woody timidly handed over the sheaf of jokes. He had written them, as usual, for David Alber; was on his way to deliver them. Watching Burrows read them can only have been an excruciating ordeal. Woody's fate lay in those few pages; in the way Burrows reacted to them: humour, particularly Woody's esoteric brand, is far from universal, as he already knew.

All Burrows knew about Woody was that he was his brother-in-law's sister's boy: Nettie Cherrie's son Alan from Brooklyn, where he came from himself. Also, according to

39

what he'd heard, he was a smart kid, already seeing his gags in print in some of the daily columns of the New York newspapers. Some press agent had him in tow, but they said he wasn't too happy about where that would lead him. Apparently, the agent's celebrity clients were getting credit for his funniest sayings, while Woody was feeding his office with them every week for a pittance.

Burrows did *not* know that his pushy young relative had found his own way to David O. Alber, the agent, while still in school. That those gags were written in moments stolen from schoolwork, or on the subway during the forty-minute ride from Avenue J station to Alber's Manhattan office. He could not have guessed what they had cost Woody in time and education lost. But he could and did recognise their power and worth. His reaction, when he read them, was explosive.

'Carie (Carie Eloise Smith, whom Burrows married in 1959) was in the next room,' he recalls. 'I shouted out to her. "Hey! Here's a young relative of mine come to see me with a whole lot of jokes he's written" – Woody'd brought me two sheets of them, all terrific – "And they're very funny! There isn't one of them I could have thought of myself!" '

Burrows asked Woody to tell him, then, about the arrangement between him and Alber. Woody let him know how the agent had given him his first professional assignment. How Earl Wilson, one of the columnists who had printed his first gags, had put the two of them in touch with one another. And how frustrated Woody was beginning to be with writing for 'only a few miserable bucks', while Wilson and other famous New York columnists – Robert Sylvester and others – were using his material free of charge from Alber's press agency, to weedle publicity for the celebrity clients he handled.

Burrows' comment must have sent him home walking on air. He says he told Woody: 'Don't worry, Alan. If you can write jokes like these you'll have no trouble. Leave this stuff with me and I'll pass it along to some of the people I know. If they pick it up, which I think they will, they'll pay *you* for it.'

He was thinking, he says, of Peter Lind Hayes and Sid Caesar, knowing their unceasing need for good, humorous writers to feed them with just the sort of stuff Woody seemed capable of providing. He still remembers and chuckles over Woody's opening joke, at the top of the first sheet. It was the one about his mother: 'She used to come into the bathroom and sink my boats' (later adapted, with less beneficial results, to his first marriage). If that wasn't funny enough for them Abe Burrows didn't know show-business.

But he did, and those jokes sold. Woody was launched.

Modestly, Abe says now: 'All I did was open the door for him. Believe me, he'd have got there on his own without my help.' And Woody no doubt recognises the debt he owes. It is part of the debt the world of those who love entertainment owes to Abe Burrows.

But Burrows was not the only one to spot Woody's potential. On 27 February 1953, when Woody was just seventeen and a quarter and with a bare four months to go to graduation, he was profiled in the school newspaper. It was a revealing portrait. At a time when Woody should have been concentrating on his schoolwork, the *Midwood Argus* noted – with sneaking admiration (in a 'spotlight' article carrying a picture of his young, intent face under the slicked-back crop of hair): 'Alan is a carrot-topped senior who has made quite a name for himself as a gag-writer. Within the past few months his quips have appeared in some twenty columns in New York newspapers . . . perhaps you've seen them? He uses the pen name of Woody Allen.'

It suggests another reason Woody may have had for choosing that particular professional name – perhaps an association of 'Midwood' with his own, given name of 'Alan'? Whatever gave it birth, he was ensuring its prominence now.

Woody was making others, apart from his classmates, laugh. How he was doing so, he could most probably not have explained. As the *Argus* spotlight writer quoted him saying: 'I just sit down at the typewriter and think funny.'

41

The article continued, 'That is Alan Konigsberg's formula for turning out a hundred gags a week . . . he claims that writing jokes is a full-time job.'

Across the years that sounds like a cry from the heart as he struggled – using only the 'native intelligence' Leonard Harrison has referred to – to make his grades with the necessary thirty-two credits for graduation, and to pass his examinations. It certainly can't have been easy. And the article continued: 'While these jokes give him experience and fame he does not get paid for them.' Since this write-up appeared after Alber's arrangement, it would seem either that the school reporter got it wrong, or that Woody regarded those weekly dollars as mere expenses – which in truth they almost were.

'To pick up money,' the writer pressed on, 'he sells sketches to comedians. His material has already been submitted to Bob and Ray, Bob Hope and Larry Storch.' But these were sketches, not gags. In retrospect it seems a pity Hope didn't pick one or two of them up. If he had, he might have gained more respect for Woody's talent; and learned from him just how deeply Woody respected his own. 'A naturally funny man.' Woody thought him. When Bob Hope came to describe Woody Allen in public, years later – an occasion when Woody had put together a biography of Hope's best film clips, then failed to show up for their presentation in New York's Lincoln Centre – he called Woody only 'half a genius'.

Woody had already performed on stage when that article in the *Argus* appeared. 'Alan,' the reporter wrote, 'sometimes exhibits his talents as a humorist before an audience . . . (he) has also learned to tap dance, play the piano, and perform many feats of magic.'

Sadly, no record of Woody's stage performances during those schooldays seems to exist. And the way his current spokesmen put it (and which all known accounts of his career to date reiterate) he first put a timid foot on the public stage during the early Sixties, some ten years later.

So gag-writing was rapidly becoming the centre of Woody's universe. It offered bread-and-butter support for the launch he dreamed of. It could take him out and away from the narrow confines of Avenue K and Flatbush. By its means he could write his way out of the shell around him, free himself from the boredom of school, poverty and domestic pressures.

As he has since shown, his love for his parents was warm and sincere. But the gulf between Woody's aims and theirs must have made even a Jewish mother's devotion irksome. And how else could he remove the gentle, misplaced encouragement coming at him from all sides to 'do something with your life, something worthwhile'? Invariably this meant passing well out of the school he was 'so lucky to be at', and spending more long years at university or college before settling, in admirable dullness, into the desired role of professional, or even religious life.

It must have seemed that his only chance of escape lay in earning sufficient money and success from gag-writing to enjoy complete independence. Yet even in doing so he would be disappointing his parents. One can imagine how any mention of this would have led to agonising discussions and entreaties in the family.

He was a clever boy! Writing and selling gags through his uncle by marriage, that was fine. But what of the future? Was he really going to risk his whole career on a few weeks' earnings of twenty-five dollars from a press agent? And promises? What good were promises in showbusiness? For a boy like him, from a good Jewish home, with a good school and university now opening its arms to him, how could he be so senseless as to throw away the golden chance he had of a *real* career – yes, as a pharmacist, why not. Or perhaps a doctor even?

It was answerable in only one way: by attaining such immediate and glittering success as he barely dreamed possible. For the time, at least, he had to bow to circumstance. Unless he was to break their hearts and risk ruining himself, there was only one thing to do about his parents' sensible wishes. He had to go to college as soon as he had graduated.

Go fight City Hall

At ten o'clock on the morning of 24 June 1953, Dr Jacob Ross opened the proceedings of what was to be his last and Woody's only graduation ceremony. The 720 graduating Seniors of Class of '53, largest in Midwood's history, listened first to a bible reading by their highest ranking girl student, Nina Zippin, then to the strains of the 'Aida March' played by the Midwood Symphonic Band.

A memorable occasion, one might have thought; though Woody, seems to have played little part in it.

By ten thirty, it was already so hot under a glazed blue, cloudless sky that many of the Seniors were gently flapping their light gowns – the girls in white, the boys in navy blue – to stir up a faint breeze. Some who had bolted breakfast and spent overlong fidgetting their way into unaccustomed clean suits and clothes – their appearances monitored by parental and family censure – were suffering waves of faintness.

When Alan Konigsberg's name was called (almost its last public appearance) it can safely be assumed that a neatly attired figure, lacking more than sixty-six inches in height but immaculate in well-pressed clothing bought specially for the occasion, strode up to receive his scroll. But did he feel that sense of pride and achievement, if not of glowing honour, to which he was entitled?

Why Woody chooses to blinker the memory of that landmark in his young life is not clear. But there are those who treasure it. 'He was such a neat little boy,' a woman relative remembers. 'And Woody's mother always saw to it that he was a credit to the family. Things were not easy for them at that particular time. But she and his father, as well as Letty his sister, must have taken great pride in Woody's graduation. They were all so anxious for him to do well.'

The school could hardly share their pride. 'Did Midwood fail, or did Woody fail us?' Midwood's present principal, Leonard Harrison wonders. 'An interesting question. You're talking about genius, and we don't understand genius. Can we even recognise it? I doubt it. In Woody's case, we did not.'

More than once Mr Harrison and his personal assistant Mrs Pearl Roberts have sent invitations to Woody to join the school in celebration of its achievements. Most recently, they invited him to the Waldorf Astoria in New York (last May, 1981) to celebrate the fortieth anniversary of Midwood's foundation. It seems he has yet to show up at these events.

'And why should *we* do all we can for them, when *he* doesn't lift a finger?' other ex-students are wont to complain. Mordy Gunty is one of these. This successful comedian, one of many Midwoodians who have achieved fame, was voicing such feelings in Florida in the spring of 1981 with some vehemence – according to ex-classmates of Woody's who heard him.

Midwood has always been, no doubt always will be, highly competitive. Mr Harrison believes this may have had a damaging effect. 'Woody just did not relate to the competitive side of life here,' he says. 'In fact, it could have intimidated him. All those pushers and joiners and shakers!'

He adds, with considerable sympathy: 'I was like that myself as a child, so I can well understand. They're terrifying! Fighting for grades and distinctions, indeed for recognition, whatever field it is in. To become eagle scouts, or any other form of achievement, they'll push everyone else aside.'

As the principal explains, the same 150 names in a school such as Midwood 'almost invariably tend to show up at the top of all that is worth attaining.' So, he says: 'there are those who just creep by, with nobody noticing.' And

Woody, in his view, was one of these.

From his windows on the main floor Mr Harrison can see the wings of the school in which nearly 2,000 young Brooklyn-ites are shaping and equipping themselves for an uncertain future. 'God knows who's in this school at the moment,' he says. 'It could be the next president of the United States! It could be another Woody Allen!'

From a transcript of his record with, attached to it, past details from the elementary Public School 99 which he had attended earlier, one can see that Mr Harrison's vision of Woody as a misfit is fully justified. He avoided contact with nearly all those involved in the arts, drama, music, journalism and sports, Woody stayed with Woody and nobody else. 'I can tell you this,' Mr Harrison confides. 'He took a full academic diploma, which is the highest there is. He didn't fail in anything. But if you look for special credits, nothing. He just made it, level. With high reading scores, too.

'Woody's problem, I'm told, was very probably simple shyness. And that would explain it. If you go back to Midwood society in the four years he was there, up until 1953, it was all very middle and upper-middle-class. They were nearly all strivers, over-achievers in that society. You can see that from their activities.

'I look at things like his IQ. His reading scores, which were high. High mathematics, too, very high. These are standardised, objective examinations of achievement and ability. His performance, on the other hand, when put to the test, was only so-so. Just enough to get by. He took Regents Examination, one of the State exams. Ultimately he graduated at a respectable level – not sixties and seventies, but better. So every indication we have shows intelligence – *and lack of any real interest in the school.*'

Midwood then offered three levels of diploma. As Mr Harrison explains, they were: 'General, for students who were not in any way gifted. Commercial, for those wanting to become stenographers and so forth. And for the academic children the highest was College Prep, which is what he took.'

With this diploma, Woody was equipped to go on to either Brooklyn College or New York University. He chose the latter, and enrolled for a course in Communication Arts. It was hardly surprising that his record lacked any great appeal to his future professors, but it was enough to gain entry.

'I'd say that, on this basis – and it's only a guess – he went through school on purely native intelligence,' Leonard Harrison surmises. 'He didn't crack a bone over it. Which is a pretty hard thing to do, and still graduate. He just relied on intelligence to do the work for him. For example, he took algebra and geometry and intermediate algebra. He took two and a half years of Hebrew. But in general I don't think he was ever one of those who showed up, or joined in. He hasn't concealed this fact, I believe. It's unfortunate but, as he says, this was just not one of the happiest times of his life.'

This *I need yet?*

At first, without the meaningless pursuit of academic learning which Midwood had imposed, Woody probably felt almost magically released. He had the freedom to see and do what he liked. Where in the past his filmgoing had been restricted to the neighbourhood cinemas, which featured his favourite comedy stars: Bob Hope, Buster Keaton and, towering over all, the (to him) riotously funny Marx Brothers, he was now not only able to see whatever he chose in the great movie-houses of Manhattan, indeed, he was obliged to do so.

This was because he (together with his friend Mickey Rose) had enrolled in a Communications Arts Course at New York University, alongside New York's Washington Square. The compromise was no doubt to pacify, if not satisfy, his parents. At least it *was* a college course. If Woody stuck it out, there was a degree at the end of it. Unfortunately, he was not to do so.

'Woody didn't always show up at college as he should have done,' Mickey Rose remembers tactfully. 'I guess he was already too busy selling his stuff and making money; so there didn't seem as much need for the course, in his case. For me, it was a very useful four years and I graduated at the end of it with a Bachelor of Arts degree.'

Not so Woody. He could not, it seems get off the academic hook fast enough. Riding up and down between Brooklyn and Washington Square he must have found time to dream. In doing so, he saw ahead of him a path which made university honours redundant. The wave of conscience which had prompted him to carry out his family's wishes, to take at least the first tottering steps towards their ideal of his becoming, eventually, a professional pharmacist or similar, probably evaporated. Everything in him seems to have rebelled against it.

That other path must have appeared infinitely more attractive. Burrows' encouragement, and Alber's ready acceptance of everything he'd written, had surely confirmed his belief that he was capable of earning a living by pen and wit? Stuffy lectures on the art of film-making could only be tedious interruptions. Though the professors were knowledgeable and distinguished, the need for their scholarly view (of the medium he already felt himself a tiny part of) simply did not exist. He craved live showbusiness.

Thus, in spite of all his earnest tutors could do (and the late Professor Gessner was a highly respected member of the NYU faculty, as was another of Woody's professors, Irving Falk), his interest in their courses lasted a bare few weeks. Thereafter, he and they probably parted company by mutual consent.

A further attempt to repay his parents, by taking a university degree at New York's City College, also failed in an even shorter time. He appears to have dropped out of both within a period of six months. Knowing how this would affect his mother, especially, it must have been a very unhappy young man who took these tidings home. Woody would not have been human if he had not felt a major wrench in having to disappoint both parents. If they still clung, in their hearts, to the vain belief that he would one day 'come to his senses' and embark on a respectable career, there was little he could say to dissuade them.

But it was a girl, the only girl who had ever shown Woody real affection and regard apart from his kid sister, who seems to have most influenced his thoughts and decisions during those bleak winter months of 1953, following graduation. Harlene Rosen was something quite special. Throughout the following year she filled Woody's horizon.

Harlene was probably more interested in the death of the French painter Henri Matisse. She was involved in the world of art, music and philosophy, enrolling on leaving school at Hunter College for a course in the last of these. Thereafter she encouraged Woody to believe it was a subject which could help him to overcome that overwhelming shyness which was still cleaving his tongue to the roof of his mouth. Indeed she persuaded him to take it up.

They had met when she was a fifteen-year-old freshman at Hunter, reading for a science degree. Her father, Julius Rosen, kept a shop in Brooklyn which, Mickey Rose remembers, sold shoes. She was a tall, attractive girl whose interest in fine art (which she still practises, professionally) was deeply sincere. Through her, Woody was lifted into a cultural orbit to which previously he had paid only the barest lip-service – the world of serious, intellectual and creative writers and artists. Also, Harlene played the piano. It meant that, with Mickey's drums and Woody's clarinet, the trio could spend wonderfully spirit-lifting hours beating out the rhythms and blues of early Dixieland jazz.

If anyone saw Woody and Harlene as ill-matched, they kept it to themselves. She was so different from the girls he had tried to ingratiate himself with at Midwood: a good listener who encouraged his growing interest in culture and the arts, as well as being pleasant-looking; an essentially nice person who seemed to all who met and knew her to be a perfect foil for his more intense moments. If she did not seem able to come anywhere near to sharing the distortions of his 'funny' views, at least she did not try to rival them, or put them down. Harlene gave Woody faith in himself while others tended to destroy it.

She also seems to have believed (perhaps too readily) almost everything he said. The tales he told, the fantasies he loved to create, she appeared to swallow them wholesale. If his humour projected outwards, with an inner core of total seriousness, hers seems to have been the converse. She showed to all who saw them together that her smiles and jokes were, if anywhere, buried deep inside her slender frame. Equally, she seems to have convinced Woody that there was almost nothing she would *not* believe, if he put it to her with sufficient insistence. 'I told her, when we were discussing why I was so keen on jazz, that I was a red-headed Negro,' Woody boasted to a close friend of those years. 'And she believed me!'

Even now, Harlene's acceptance of such a tale sounds strange; but it would explain her later distress, when she discovered how he had used her as a butt for his jokes. In Woody's defence it has to be said that he has never seen his mockery of those close to him – not even of his mother and father – as in any way indelicate or hurtful, provided that it has been in the natural expression of his art.

Harlene, for all that she may have lacked the highly eccentric comedy of Woody's restless mind, was a refreshing companion after the rough handling he had had from the Midwood co-eds. They were, as he later explained, mainly blue-stocking types: deeply involved in philosophical studies, way-out artistic pursuits and causes. They wanted to drag him in. And when they found Woody shrinking from the activist areas of political, social and artistic life, recoiling in horror from marches, demos and all the furious engineering of protest about one thing or another, they seem to have dropped him with mild contempt.

So Harlene was an oasis. And as Woody's career burgeoned, thrusting him into contact with a disturbing world of equally self-seeking, heartless men and women, it seems she was the one he turned to almost exclusively. It is easy to see how these circumstances, and her steady loyalty, led to a deepening of the love between them; and eventually to marriage.

By this time, he was fully embarked on a writing career. The big William Morris Agency had taken him under their prestigious wing. Aware of his potential talent through first Alber and then Burrows, they had offered to represent him while he was still riding the subway up and down to Manhattan from Flatbush, pouring his creative energies into one-line throwaways and sketches.

Having signed him, they found him a job: a junior post in the Writers' Development Program of America's leading television network, NBC. And at a dazzling $175 a week. The sole drawback, as he was to learn, was that it would take him to Hollywood.

In prospect, the idea may have seemed attractive. Hollywood was the summit of success for working writers, and for those – like Woody – in television it was beginning to offer increasingly wide horizons. Burbank's TV colour studios were moving into full-scale production and an exciting number of shows had been scheduled. The place was a hive of fresh, vigorous talent.

Yet it affected Woody like leg irons. From what he has often said, it's clear that Hollywood and he are the opposite of soul-mates. He felt trapped. Whether it was the blatant opportunism of many of its incumbents, or the ecological poison of its smog, has never been explained: certainly he hated the place and its false values.

One does not know, of course, how much rejection of his essentially east-coast, New York humour played a part. Or if his more senior colleagues on the Writers' Program were unappreciative. These were the nursery days of colour production in TV, and novelty was a dangerous commodity to attempt. Woody's unique individuality may have, and probably did, alarm those moguls of the small screen whose greatest nightmare was to see audience ratings drop through incomprehension.

All we know is that Woody set to work because that was what he in his innocence believed was how one justified any contract. What he may have overlooked, was the extraordinary double and treble thinking, the fear and falsehood, of the film colony in the grip of colour television mania. Alone for the first time, or at least for the first period without relatives and familiar neighbourhood faces, what could be more natural than that he should discover a vital need for Harlene's support and loving companionship?

This was a high-intensity epoch in Hollywood, with Marilyn Monroe perched like a Christmas tree fairy on top of the pyramid of tinselly stars – Tony Curtis, Rock Hudson, Robert Mitchum among a host of others. The boulevards at night were thronged with young hopefuls, drawn to the magnet of 'stardom'. Every bar held its contingent of disappointed tyros, divorcees and would-be suicides.

And Woody did not take to it. Not at all. If anything, he found the few months he spent there infinitely less agreeable than Flatbush – Brooklyn at least held real people, however cloying and intrusive; these were spiritual zombies.

Harlene must have heard his cry for help, translated into a marriage proposal by long-distance telephone, and hurried across the American continent. For both of them crossing the Rockies for the first time held a significance not far removed from crossing a joint Rubicon.

As Woody has since explained, passionately and sincerely, Hollywood was merely another Midwood: teeming with pushy over-ambitious joiners and 'get-with-it' operators. Offering work there could be a frustrating experience for even the most talented writer. And the terror thumping at the heart of the film kingdom as television viewing-figures rose from week to week, was making it a creative cripple-park. Movie writers were manically striving to soothe the panicked breasts of producers who knew only one yardstick of success: box-office returns.

Having been through other problems with him, Harlene no doubt found this familiar ground. She had not only been with Woody when he enrolled at New York University on leaving Midwood, but also when he had been ejected from his course there through 'lack of interest and attendance.' Also, when New York's City College course had ended the same way, she had smoothed Woody's ruffled conscience, restoring his self-confidence as little else could have done.

What mattered now was that he needed her once more. And Hollywood had shown how great that need was. Woody was barely nineteen, and already there were two failed college courses behind him. Ahead was the hope, still struggling towards the light (as when he had confessed it to the school newspaper), to learn enough about the workings of the film or television world to be able to take an executive part in one of them. Perhaps, even, as the personal director of the ideas for films and plays which kept tumbling about in his head. Nothing could have been more natural than for him to believe that Harlene, rather more than anyone else he had ever known, was fitted to help him attain this fulfilment. Her cool balance and cultural stance had revealed glimpses of a world that must have been new to him. It was a world of distinguished, non-materialistic artists who valued creative work in place of money. Set against the vulgarity and self-seeking of Hollywood, and inflamed by the difficulties he felt in communicating with this alien world, there can have been little doubt in Woody's mind which of the two held the greater attraction for him.

His need was for a more discerning and sensitive medium in which to work. Harlene no doubt seemed the ideal person to help him satisfy it.

What girl could have resisted the proposal whispered across 3,000 miles of telephone wire? Woody's imploring voice . . . his request that Harlene fly over and marry him in California immediately . . . Of course she agreed. At the rushed ceremony in the now untraceable Hollywood Hawaiian hotel she seems to have given her age as sixteen, though she now says she believes she was a year older. Either way, she was far too young to read the signs.

Once Woody was married, all strings tying him to the respectable confines of Avenue K, and the Brooklyn apartment house his family had moved to at Number 1402, were severed. Marriage gave him total independence. After a few more weeks of tolerating the film colony atmosphere, he brought his bride back east. It must have seemed only natural for him to acquire his first rented Manhattan apartment, half an hour's subway ride from Flatbush, and to settle into the role of a breadwinning, salaried staff-writer.

Harlene went back to college. Woody, to keep in step with her cultural development, has told how he studied her subject, philosophy, privately at home. It's doubtful if it taught him as much as the man who instructed him learned from their lessons together.

Both he and she were having to make heavy adjustments to their ways of life in living together. Hers must have required unusual tolerance: Woody, by all accounts, was not without individual characteristics. His eating habits could be described as defensive rather than aggressive. He seems to have liked only food he was assured would not taste strange, or exotic. His clothes may have been something of a problem too, in that he chose everything he wore with considerable care to avoid what was rough, or irritating, to his sensitive skin. And often without regard to colour or pattern.

Worse still must have been his addiction to solitude and city life. It can only have forced her to select those entertainments and social engagements which fitted in with his sensitive demands.

As yet, little open conflict seems to have appeared between them. To close friends, they appeared fully integrated. Mickey Rose was often with them. 'They were like any other stable, married couple at that time,' he remembers. 'We'd go to restaurants and ball games. Or we'd watch ice hockey on Sundays in Madison Square Garden, rooting for the New York Rangers. It was all pretty normal and uneventful.'

Rose says he never entertained the slightest suspicion that anything was wrong with the marriage. Thinking back, he says: 'They didn't go around holding hands, or anything. And I suppose you could say they didn't demonstrate much open affection. But you wouldn't have expected it. Harlene was always a quiet, introspective and very serious girl as I recall. They seemed to get along perfectly well when I saw them. It just never occurred to me that they'd break up.'

Early on it seemed that it never occurred to Woody, either. Harlene was undemanding. She appears to have respected his need to work at his writing. She helped him practise his clarinet, accompanying him on piano whenever one was available. And they shared a fascination and enthusiasm for those new, satirical comedians coming into prominence with biting force: Mort Sahl and Lenny Bruce. 'We were all greatly influenced by several of them around that time, especially Mort Sahl,' Mickey Rose says.

55

'Woody was encouraging me to write. I think people we saw performing in Greenwich Village and around New York gave me a lot of help.'

The idea began to be tossed around that the two of them might write together. It was the kind of late-evening optimism echoed by dozens of young writers. But Woody was never one to let ideas fly out of the window without a serious attempt to make them work. As he has done for so many close friends so many times since, he acted as a vehicle for Mickey Rose in more senses than one. Rose is the first to admit that he owes his marriage to Woody.

'Yes, Woody fixed up a blind date for me. Through Harlene, I met my wife (Judy Wolf, as she was then) that night. She and Harlene were classmates at Hunter College. We married when I was twenty-five, and we've all been friends ever since.'

Since the Roses' date was not a foursome, Woody and Harlene did not see the romance blossom. But they had plenty of opportunity to watch its development. The four friends spent as many evenings and weekends together as they could afford. Working at NBC was demanding, and whenever possible Woody was augmenting his slender pay by writing assignments outside. Everybody seemed pleased with the way things were going – except for those relatives in Brooklyn who complained that Woody so seldom paid them a visit. For some of these, the profession he was in was too risky to suggest that he should be left alone to get on with it.

So, from day to day and week to week, Woody went on writing the same quick-fire, funny material he had always written. It went into the mouths and acts of comedians on the *Ed Sullivan Show*, *The Tonight Show* and others in the NBC repertoire. Carol Channing was fed his lines as one of the network's more privileged artists. There were many other, less distinguished beneficiaries who never knew how lucky they were to be presented with such hilarious material.

It was, in some ways, a treadmill. But he had the facility to write almost to order. And if a litttle exploitation of Woody's innocence took place, at least he was learning while earning his meagre crust. In the early Fifties, even in Manhattan, it was possible to live reasonably comfortably in rented accommodation on less than $200 a week, which was what NBC still paid him. The only drawback to this was that Woody had engaged an expensive, highly professional promoter of talent who charged a high price for his services. This was an agent on the staff of another agency who had an eye to setting up on his own. He persuaded Woody to become one of his first clients and at the time it no doubt seemed a good move.

Nobody could have foreseen the swift acceleration of Woody's rising star. The agent, Harvey Meltzer had signed him to an exclusive contract under which, it has since been reported, he was to receive twenty-five per cent – a quarter – of everything the comedian and writer earned from his work. Meltzer was to promote him. The arrangement was binding for a full five years, during which Woody's income rose to the point where Meltzer was receiving more than initially had been paid to them both.

The contract ran until 1958, at which time Woody was reported to be receiving fees amounting to some $2,000 a week: Meltzer thereby would have taken $500 without stirring further than the bank. But in the early days he had done everything in his power to promote Woody, and his early faith deserved its reward. It also bore fruit in a highly important way for Woody's career and private life, though this may have been accidental. Through Harvey Meltzer, Woody was introduced to one of America's great showmen, Max Liebman.

Meltzer sent Woody to see Liebman when the impresario was putting together a new show starring the popular comedian Buddy Hackett. Max Liebman is a tiny, frail-looking man with a disarmingly quiet, mild manner. His shrewd eye for talent is renowned for having discovered many stars including Danny Kaye. He is also the originator of the television *Muppets* and founder of one of America's longest-running TV series, *Your Show of Shows*. He admits with a twinkle in his old eye to being seventy-nine, but his memory of Woody's arrival in his office and studio at 130

West 56th Street on that September day in 1956 is as clear as crystal. 'This guy who was head of the department for comedy writers at NBC and had been with the William Morris Agency called me up,' he recalls. ' "I've got a young man here I'd like to send you," he told me. "Maybe you could use him on the Hackett Show?" '

' "Certainly," I told him. At that time I had Danny Simon, Neil Simon's brother, working on the show which was the first situation comedy I'd ever been connected with. I was having to buy scripts in from outside. So I was looking for anybody at all who represented himself as a comedy writer.'

When Woody took the creaking elevator up to Max Liebman's rooms he can have had no idea how desperate Max was to hire writing talent; indeed, any talent which could produce material for his show. The door opened to show a man who, even to Woody, seemed small. But his welcome was brief, quiet and affirmative. 'You can start right away,' Max told him, 'and all I want to see from you is material that's funny. I don't care what it's about, but make me laugh!'

Max Liebman takes up the story: 'He came in and told me his name was Woody Allen. That was about as much as he said. I put him right to work, and he would come up to the studio above my office and sit there all day, maybe going out for a sandwich at lunchtime. Nothing more. We'd have discussions, then he'd just turn out the stuff every day.'

A look of remembered surprise crosses his face. 'And hardly a word out of him! A "good morning" when he came in, and a "good night" when he left. We didn't converse at all – I began to wonder if he was dumb!'

Max was going through an early love affair with television, in which he tried to involve his writers. As he says: 'I was *devoted* to live television. You see, I was trying to put on the one and only sit-com being done live. It took a lot of exceptionally good material because there could be no re-takes or cuts. It *had* to work first time.'

Daily, he would urge Woody and the others to fit their talents into the mould he was seeking to perfect. 'Woody would listen, nod, then go away that night and come in next day with reams of paper. I got the impression he'd been working half the night. But it wasn't right! It wasn't what I wanted for the show!'

There are few quieter, less bullying producers than Max Liebman. And few who knew so absolutely and unshakeably when material, or performance, lacked the pitch and quality he sought. Ask him now what was absent from Woody's painstaking contributions and he doesn't hesitate.

'Why wasn't his work right for the Buddy Hackett Show? I can identify it exactly, definitely I can. Woody Allen writes well *only for himself*. That's why.'

Max Liebman pronounces his verdict with experienced assurance. His voice and manner are so quiet and undemonstrative it's hard to believe he is looking back on a failure he still regrets. Or that his clear reflections span a quarter of a century, the time that has slipped away since Woody tried to give him what he wanted. There is no hint of bitterness or condemnation in his criticism: it is the one hundred per cent professional assessment of a master showman.

'The best writing Woody ever did was for himself. Time has proved that over and over again,' he says firmly. 'He just couldn't write what I wanted for Hackett because, as I soon realised, he is really only best suited when he has himself in mind. Totally.'

He spreads pale, self-deprecating hands. 'All right,' he admits, begging the question. 'The Buddy Hackett show was not a great success. And after twenty or so shows it disappeared. But it wasn't until much later that I realised why Woody hadn't been able to match his talents to it, that was when I saw him doing a stand-up monologue at Max Gordon's Blue Angel in Manhattan.'

He smiles at the memory. 'One day,' he says. 'I read in *Variety* that among the new acts opening at Max Gordon's place was this comedian. His name was Woody Allen, and it described his act. I said to myself, isn't that funny? Two guys with the same name!

'Then I bumped into Max Gordon in the street. I said: "Max, I just read you've a new comedian down there. Is he a slight fellow with red hair, doesn't weigh much more than 120 pounds?"

'He said, "Yes, that's the fellow. Woody Allen."

'I said: "You mean he talks?"

'He said: "Oh yeah. He talks well."

'I said: "Isn't that amazing? I thought he was dumb!" '

Sometimes when Woody was working for Liebman the producer would walk a few blocks with him on his way home. He says now that, aside from the show and the need he had – which Woody was not filling – for material for it, he had grown to like his silent writer. The fact is Liebman was curious to know more about him.

'I found him interesting,' Max Liebman admits. 'Not in the stuff he wrote, but in himself. I knew he was funny. But it was the wrong kind of funny for the show, which was very broad.'

Thinking back, Liebman surmises: 'We were trying to do farce and I guess he was writing light comedy. That may have been the trouble.'

He nods, in agreement with himself at last, as if he's found something long lost. 'I'll tell you,' he says. 'Woody's material then had that personal tinge to it, which came from right inside him. He wasn't anybody else but himself when he was projecting it.

'My own analysis of his development is that he was a complete professional as a writer, and an amateur as a performer.

'He was portraying himself as, I would say, an untutored *nebbish*. That means, in the lingo, a young, inept person. He wanted to show himself as an actor who'd been schooled professionally but not intellectually.

'Nevertheless, of all the young comedians practising their craft at that time – Mort Sahl included – he was one of the very few who had an intellectual tinge to his vocabulary and language.

'Sahl was not autobiographical, more an outside commentator on the political scene. And Lenny Bruce was accenting something else, entirely different from Woody Allen. He had a touch of what Woody had a lot of.

'That was schooling. And having been a college grad. He could be categorised, I think, as a young intellectual dealing with the problems he encounters in order to survive the period he was existing in.

'Remember, this was the period when we were beginning to be affected by the generation gap. When the young were coming out against old people they believed had led the world into a mess. They felt at a loss as to where they were going, or where they came from. And Woody was one of those who had a message they could understand.

'You see, they'd created a gulf between themselves and the Establishment. Because that was what they blamed for sending them abroad to fight unpopular wars, as cannon-fodder for causes they didn't believe in.

'Woody came from that background. He started out – definitely, but *definitely* – as a cult entertainer. And those young, uncertain people were the cult. That was how he started to get acceptance from them.'

The old head nods sagely. For Max Liebman, Woody is more than just a comic writer he once employed. He is a social and intellectual phenomenon. The faint voice starts up again, the thin hands gesturing faintly:

'Woody Allen,' he says, 'would have competed in any period. For instance, he is more of the Establishment than Mort Sahl was. Mort Sahl was not of the new breed like Woody, he definitely belonged to the old, traditional pattern of the American political critic. He went back to the American cowboy and the Wild West; to Will Rogers, who was a political philosopher commenting on the political scene before anything else: *and* part of the Establishment.

'Woody was not like that at all. He wasn't an anti-Establishment personality. He was just involved in what he saw as entertaining and amusing from his own, particular point of view.

'His talent was in being intellectually funny – and it is on a different plane from comedy. Usually wit is in the printed word rather than the performing arts, but he had that

61

combination. And, up to the time he worked for me, whatever he did was for *him*. For what I'd call the commercial segment of the comedy world.'

The old showman, who saw down into the roots of some of the greatest comedy entertainers of our generation, thus consigns Woody to posterity, and the success his unaided talents were to achieve. His genius had created one of America's most popular holiday playgrounds: at Tamiment in Pennsylvania. And it was here that Woody was to take his most important step forward.

You want I should sing, too?

If as the old saying goes, good American millionaires go to Paris when they die, less successful New Yorkers may be lucky enough to end up in Pennsylvania's summer camp in the Pocono Mountains, Tamiment. For those who take a holiday there it is still a haven of relaxation and beauty as well as fun. And when Woody and Harlene had the good fortune to work at the camp for three hot summers, when the sidewalks of their city streets were practically molten, the place was a writer's paradise.

Woody had been working his heart out in Manhattan for Liebman. The unsuccessful struggle to integrate his low-profile comedy with the broad *slapschtik* of Buddy Hackett would seem, in Max Liebman's recollection, to have taken a heavy toll. If rewards had been greater he might have managed to afford a holiday. Both Woody and Harlene badly needed one. But as things were this was out of the question.

Then one day a showman friend of Max's, Moe Hack, offered him a season at Tamiment as a resident writer with free accommodation and board for both Woody and his wife. Hack had worked for Liebman when old Max (young Max then) was shaking off his Viennese past and laying the foundations for a long, successful career in American showbusiness. Liebman had taken on directorship of Tamiment, later handing it on to Moe Hack. When he mentioned Woody to him as a writer for his stable, Hack did not hesitate. As he says: 'If Max said he was funny and a hard worker, that was good enough for me. I had to produce too many shows down there to worry about the finer points.'

And Woody, despite the dislike he has expressed publicly, on TV and in interviews, for open-air, sun-soaking holidays, seems to have seized the offer with delight. It was, after all, a wonderful break, coming at an ideal time. It meant he could get out of the rut he was in with Max, while at the same time providing him and Harlene with a change of scene. Tamiment at capacity housed 1,500 vacationing New Yorkers, mainly from well-to-do Jewish families. The women competed in showing off their discount mink stoles and flashy jewellery, the men their Palm Beach seersucker and panama hats. Cigars, scent and jazzy swimsuits were in profitable demand, and the accent was heavily on entertainment round the clock – preferably loud, hilarious and non-stop.

Any comedy writer could work there with a guarantee of acceptance for even his weaker lines and jokes. And Woody was not just any writer. Tamiment, Max Liebman told him, was just what his talent needed. It would provide a unique setting for his wildest, funniest gags and situations.

And, as no doubt he soon learned, it was also a place which show and variety people had learned to love like a powerful drug.

Liebman had got it out of his system by the time Woody went to work for him in '56. More than twenty years had passed since he'd taken over as social director at Tamiment in the pre-war hot summer of 1934, years in which he'd created a formula for the guests which included music, vaudeville, a nightclub revue and movies. And which reached a crescendo on Saturday nights with the Big Show of the Week.

He'd written sketches, produced acts, handled lighting, music, and supervised costumes and wardrobe. On top of all that he'd cast the shows. And his greatest talent had always been picking unknowns and making them into stars, which was fortunate for Woody.

In 1938, when Max Liebman had been at Tamiment for four seasons running, he had already found and launched a comedian called Sid Caesar. Then he'd hired an assistant to write some of the sketches and gags for him: Sylvia Fine.

PUBLIC SCHOOL
99
CLASS OF
JUNE 1949

Previous page: Public School 99, Class of June 1949, Alan Konigsberg is seated in the middle of the front row.
Above: Midwood High School. (TONY MARSHALL)
Top right: Woody's entry in the Midwood Graduation Year Book, Class of 53. (TONY MARSHALL)
Bottom right: Mickey Rose's entry in the Year Book. (TONY MARSHALL)

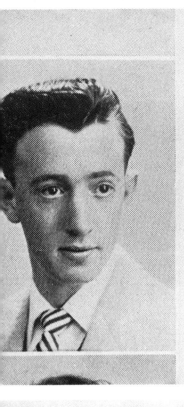

KONISBERG, ALAN
1402 Avenue K

KORNBERG, MARIL

ROSE, MICHAEL
198 Carroll Street
Varsity Baseball, '52-53; H.R.
ec'y; Visual Aids Squad;
Cafe. Squad; Hebrew Cul-
ure Club; Chem. Lab Squad.

ROSEN, ROBERT
470 Ocean Parkway
Guard Squad; H.R. Vice

Left: David O. Alber who paid Woody $25 a week to write gags while he was still a schoolboy. (KIM SPANOGH)

Below: In his first apartment admiring a newly acquired painting by Gloria Vanderbilt, 1966.
(UNITED PRESS INTERNATIONAL)

Right: At work in his East Side apartment, 1966.
(UNITED PRESS INTERNATIONAL)

Top: With Lou Jacobi rehearsing Woody's play *Don't Drink the Water,* 1966. (UNITED PRESS INTERNATIONAL)
Bottom: In his first movie *What's New Pussycat?* with Romy Schneider and Peter O'Toole. (NEW YORK POST)

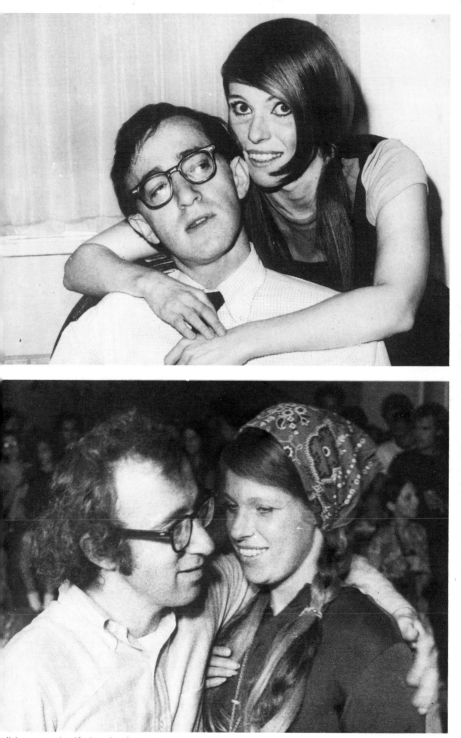

With second wife Louise Lasser. (NEW YORK POST)

Top: With Lauren Bacall supporting Jimmy Carter, 1976. (NEW YORK POST)
Bottom: With Leonard Bernstein at a New York party, 1977.
(UNITED PRESS INTERNATIONAL)

She also worked with a small revue company in a converted barn, which she persuaded Max to come and see. There was a young comedian there, she said, who was outstanding.

His name was Danny Kaye.

Max only had to watch him come on to know that Danny was a genius. When he'd signed a grateful Kaye to a season at Tamiment (which indirectly led to Sylvia and him marrying), Max had done the summer camp its first great service. His second was in persuading Moe Hack to take over when he gave up running the entertainment side of the camp. Moe was one of the most energetic and creatively stimulating directors, and he saw the value of Woody's talents.

As he says: 'Woody was a terrific find, a great asset, from the day he started with me down there at Tamiment. He and his wife, Harlene, were with us for three years, as I recall. He'd been writing for television since being thrown out of City College, New York. And gags for some newspaper columnists, I believe. He told me he wanted to be a performer.'

So all those years ago, in about 1957, Woody was voicing a desire to put his feet as well as his words on the open stage. Moe Hack won't be shaken on that point, whatever Woody's current publicists say. 'He would only do things for me he could perform in,' Moe says. 'Woody came to see me in New York when I was setting up the show for the coming season. I'd heard about him, of course. Somebody in Brooklyn had mentioned to me that there was this kid down there who wrote gags while in High School.

'When I saw how funny he could be on paper I decided to give him a chance. But I'd no idea what he could do on the stage.'

Moe was taking a gamble. Woody wasn't experienced. In his eyes, he was a green kid as likely to go clean over the heads of the relaxed, vacationing audience at Tamiment as to tickle their sense of humour.

'As it turned out, he was very funny and audiences thought so too,' he says. 'I got to be very fond of him. But to me he was always an individual.'

Writers' conferences at Tamiment were held in Moe Hack's office. There was a table at one end round which all the writers and the director would crowd, smoking and sipping iced water to combat the heat. 'Woody never would sit at the table,' Moe Hack recalls. 'He'd walk about all the time, pacing up and down. He kept thinking up ideas and firing them at us off the top of his head. His stuff was always very funny, but sometimes it struck me as weird.'

Weird or not, he had Moe in stitches. By the time Christopher Hewett, English actor and director, came to direct Woody's final season down there in 1959, he and Harlene were established favourites with the company, the audiences, and especially with Moe Hack and his daughter Paula – now Mrs Paula Cohen – who worked along with him.

Harlene, in fact, had made herself so useful and pleasant that Moe had offered her work as his secretary and typist. It was a job she was happy to take on, both for the extra dollars it put in their joint account and for the way it filled her otherwise empty days.

'I'd given them both a room and bathroom in the main complex where I had my office,' Moe explains. 'Paula was in another of these, while I and my late wife had a separate place to live. I only went in there during the daytime. It worked well because Harlene was a very nice, well-brought up young lady, obviously from a good family, and educated. So she was a bonus for me. We got along just fine.'

Moe kept Harlene fully occupied with long and repeated retyping of scripts, among them (no doubt) some of Woody's. These were always needed in the greates possible hurry. 'She was an efficient girl,' he remembers. 'Maybe not tops as a secretary, but a great help to me. She didn't show her feelings much. And she could take a lot of punishment.'

At Tamiment, where the accent was on free love and plenty of it, ('you couldn't walk across the golf course at night without tripping over them,' remembers Christopher Hewett) Harlene's punishment was of a different kind. One of their closest colleagues laughs at the notion that the split widening under the feet of their marriage was cleft by any adventures on Woody's part. As he explains: 'We were working too hard to think of anything like that.'

The man who says that is Woody's old buddy Fred Ebb, then one of the other writers at Tamiment. This highly successful lyricist (of *Cabaret,* and the recent Lauren Bacall Broadway hit, *Woman of the Year*) should know. So what he and others who were there at that time find hard to understand is why Woody and Harlene's marriage lasted no more than the five years it did. Or why Woody gave Harlene cause to feel he was slighting her in his act as soon as the break-up was final.

The way Christopher Hewett remembers it, the Allens were a quiet, happy pair. 'They shared a cabin, and used to sit out and play their recorders together in the evenings. I don't believe they went out of the camp much, if at all. They both seemed quite satisfied to be in there and working.'

Not that there was an abundance of free time, with the two sketches and one direction Moe had contracted Woody to do weekly, and Harlene's secretarial chores. Since he did not play his clarinet in the domestic area, and Harlene could not always find an accessible piano, recorders made a joint and pleasing compromise.

Yet there were no obvious signs of frustration. Hewett says he never noticed any friction between them. At night, after the audience had crept away to sleep with their partners (or somebody else's), Woody occasionally found energy enough to sit in with the resident band. These musicians, hired for the season, were good friends of the company; Hewett recalls Woody climbing on the stand with them more than once. So his domestic problems can hardly have stemmed from musical starvation; of that Hewett is certain.

As for Moe Hack and his daughter Paula Cohen, they suspected nothing. Proximity brought them closer than anyone else in the camp to Woody and Harlene. And they have tried many times to think back to the root of the Allens' separation. Yet they still find it hard to explain.

67

Paula liked Harlene. While never getting to know her intimately, there was a quality of quiet helpfulness about her which appealed to her as it did to many others there at the time. 'My recollection is that she was always very pleasant and sweet, and that she believed absolutely in Woody,' Paula says. 'Where the trouble started, I think, was when he began performing as an actor, a live comedian.

'She'd never thought of him as a performer, out there in public before a real, paying audience. They could be rough at times, which probably upset Woody a lot. And Harlene had to handle it.

'Also, I think when she'd married him she was looking forward to a husband who would be more of an intellectual type, which Woody could be. As a performer he somehow lowered himself in her eyes. It would have been all right for him to be a doctor on television, or a lawyer in open court. But this was too glaring a public stage for her. And in a way it may have offended her idea of the social class she came from, the one she felt they both belonged to.'

Moe has a more masculine view. Yet he too sees the rift as stemming from the different directions they were taking in life. Harlene was an artist, her heart and soul in the aesthetic values and finer shades of being. To Woody, it seemed, nothing was immune from use as backdrops for his comedy.

As Moe puts it: 'I guess the trouble was that she didn't have any contact with the world Woody was moving into. She didn't *want* to have any. And she made no effort to do so.' Harlene, from what little she says, would disagree, but Moe Hack saw a lot of them both. 'They were a happy enough couple on the surface,' he continues. 'But he was always trying to be funny; that was his life. I don't think she could level with him in that.'

Even then, though Moe still wonders over it, Harlene gave no sign that the schism was so deep. The Allens came to Tamiment together and they left together. Their divorce, one of those Mexican quickies, didn't happen until several months in the future. And meanwhile, there was a whole life to be lived down there, from the first day of June till

Labour Day. Then in Manhattan, with friends like Mickey Rose, for the rest of the year.

Woody and Harlene must very soon have realised that they had married before either of them had fully grown up. It was a folk singer acquaintance of Woody's, Dick Davy – a Tamiment sketch writer for a while – who sensed the true weight of their marriage burden. He remembers how it seemed to irk Woody to 'play husband', while so much else was going on. Apparently having to keep Harlene company, a young woman who had little time for the company of scriptwriters, was sometimes an unwelcome chore. 'He'd be sitting around a lunchroom and it would be time to leave,' Davy told Phil Berger (*The Last Laugh* – Morrow, 1975). 'And he'd say, "well, I've got to go back to the cabin and do the husband bit."'

To Davy, that sounded merely funny. But to many of those who knew Woody and worked with him then, anything that came out of his mouth was. Davy continued, to Berger: 'He'd say about how he got married for the first time when he was seventeen to a girl named Harlene – she was always called "Mrs Woody" – and they didn't know anything about sex. So they went to a marriage counsellor, or a rabbi, before they got married, to tell them what to do about it.'

It is not hard to detect prankster Woody's leg-pull in this story. But let Davy tell it as he remembers him saying it: 'The rabbi says "All you do is mount her like a young bull!" That's Woody telling it, and to hear him say it . . . it's just like real funny. I remember the phrase . . .'

It does seem that Woody would have turned even private thoughts into a gag to get a laugh at that time, when in the company of friends or colleagues. But this does not sound like the level of his humour and one wonders if Davy's memory of the incident (which occurred many years before he reported it in a magazine interview) is wholly accurate? However, he has more to tell us.

'Another time,' Davy reportedly said, 'I asked to talk to him. And he said "well, where will we talk?" And I said "well, I'm out there playing the guitar by the lake, like in the afternoon!" And it was the first time all summer that he'd been out there.'

For a young man as keen as Woody was on tennis and keeping fit, and with Harlene always pleased to enjoy the sights and sound of the beautiful neighbourhood, that also sounds strange. Nevertheless, as Davy recalls:

'The main thing they do at resorts (like Tamiment) is lay around on chaise-longues with their music and their gin and the water-melons. Making out. And he looks at it like it's a scene from a strange movie.

'And he got all excited! "Is this what goes on here all day, all those naked women? Wow! Why, you must have a ball. Wow!" And he's looking at all these girls. And he was like very uncomfortable. All his fantasies . . . a fish out of water, looking around. 'Cause he's always writing. He had stacks of spearmint gum. You know, for the nervousness and writing?' Naiveté and nervousness, hand in hand apparently.

'Harlene too was very shy,' Paula remembers, 'though I believe she had some other job in the city during the winter, and I know she helped my father a lot, and was paid, but very little, for doing it. We lived alongside one another but I never really got to know her, or Woody, well. They kept pretty much to themselves, which seemed to me understandable.'

Paula actually witnessed that first professional performance of Woody's in a sketch called 'Psychological Warfare'. He'd no doubt written it himself, she says. But appearing in it was an accident and not, as Moe believes, Woody's intention.

'Normally one of the actors in the company would go on and do Woody's sketches,' Paula recalls, 'but this time the guy supposed to play the main part must have got sick or something. At the last minute nobody could be found who knew the lines. Except, of course, Woody himself.

'So he went on. That I do know. Really thrown onto the stage, you might say, because up to then he'd been strictly a writer, and a very funny one.'

Paula was working as projection assistant in the camp

70

cinema, having trained and worked at the job professionally elsewhere. As a teacher now, of emotionally disturbed
teenagers, she looks back on Tamiment in those early days
with warmth. Her feelings about Woody and Harlene are
no doubt coloured by this.

'I used to see quite a lot of them in the bungalow which
the theatre staff shared. They had two rooms and shared a
bathroom. Everybody in the company loved Woody, and
not only for his work. He was always very kind to
everyone.'

Yet there were signs, she noticed, that the neuroses
which later became such a hallmark of Woody's celebrity
image were already present.

'I'd say, looking back on it, that Woody was something of
a hypochondriac even then,' she says. 'But the way he
worried about his health was really funny, because I don't
remember him ever actually being sick. While Harlene,
who never complained, was probably more often down
with a chill or something. She was healthy enough, but of
the two of them I'd say she was more prone to catching any
infection that happened to be around than he was.'

Summing up, Paula gives a shrewd assessment of
Woody's relationship with Harlene during those summers
which filled such a large part of their five years of marriage.
'Harlene,' she says, 'seemed to me to be a substitute for
Woody's mother. She gave him constant bolstering, which
he needed a lot of. He had a very low personal image.'

She adds, thoughtfully: 'Yes, at that time I'd have said
Woody would have been the most astonished person on
earth if anyone had offered him praise for his work. He
simply didn't rate himself at all, except in his writing. That
was the only thing he ever showed any real self-confidence
about. I guess because he knew he was good, which he very
definitely was.'

But if Harlene had taken over from Woody's mother in
some ways, Nettie shared some of their time at Tamiment.
Moe Hack remembers both Woody's parents well. He says
that Woody's father, Marty, made a presentation medal for
one of the competitive sporting events at Tamiment (Moe's

71

memory fails him as to which one it was), and talked proudly of his skill in the engraving of precious metals. 'They were a very nice couple,' Moe recalls, 'and meeting them it was clear to me that Woody's home life had been comfortable and pleasant. He hadn't had to struggle, that's for sure. The Konigsbergs were what I'd call respectable folk, and any children of theirs would have been brought up the right way, I'm certain of that.'

Moe, too, remembers Woody's marriage break-up. 'They'd been childhood sweethearts,' he says. 'But that doesn't always work when you get out into the mainstream of life. I think they just grew apart. And then, later, he said some things about her in public which she thought unkind, and of course that made things worse.'

But Harlene gave Moe very little hint of whatever distress lay at her heart. 'I didn't get any sign from her at all,' he says. 'She just left me at about that time and I don't believe I ever saw her again. I remember her as cool and capable, never flustered by anything and, as I say, a great help to me. I'm sorry her marriage with Woody didn't work out, but who knows about these things?'

Maybe nobody, and sometimes not even the pair involved. But Moe does have a thought or two about what went wrong as far as Tamiment was concerned, and the part it played in ending the marriage. 'I guess,' he says wisely, 'that the trouble really was that she just wasn't the right kind of wife for a guy who sees life, and humour, the way Woody sees it. For her, it must sometimes have seemed like being tied to one of those jokey distorting mirrors. And when he got into a whole new crowd down there, with all the writers and players, she wasn't game for that at all.'

Moe explains: 'I suppose I *did* see they were moving away from each other after a while. He was moving around with a whole lot of new friends and some of them may not have been good for him. I don't mean girls, he didn't have any time for them as far as I could see at that time. But show-business people. And Harlene didn't like theatre or show-business, I don't believe. She found it all too much for her.'

He adds ruminatively: 'Maybe she felt she was losing Woody to his work, which I think she was.'

The work, and the new friends, were in abundance. Both Chris Hewett and Fred Ebb look back on Tamiment with grateful tenderness. 'It was a marvellous place,' Ebb says, 'and wonderfully useful. Woody and I worked together as writers for the show and it stretched us to the limit, which was good. We didn't get paid or anything – except that Woody was paid something by Lenny Maxwell, for whom he wrote most of his material. We just got room and board. But as a place to work out, with ready-made audiences, it was very much like attending a course in sketch writing under pressure. And it was supposed in those days to be something of an honour as a writer to be asked to go there.'

Fred spent the whole of that last 1959 summer with Woody. He became very fond of him, both as a person and a talented co-worker. He found Harlene 'nice' but less interesting. 'Naturally, Woody and I were much closer,' he explains. 'She was very sweet and all that, but we were having to work together day after day. Actually, I'd say that what struck me most about Harlene was how quiet she was, almost like a little mouse. She was quite attractive though, with a very good, slim figure, and Woody must have seen something in her. They seemed genuinely fond of each other.'

The night Fred Ebb went to dinner with them both, he found himself watching a real-life performance such as later audiences would find hilarious in Woody's films. 'Harlene didn't appear, she had flu or something,' Fred remembers. 'So he had to make the dinner.

'He'd bought a chicken. He put it on the spit of the rotisserie oven, which was okay. But everything Woody did was funny, even cooking that chicken. I can't explain why, any more than I can explain what it was that made me have to fight the laughs when he was on stage with me. But I do know I've remembered that meal to this day, and always with a lot of pleasure. Woody didn't mean it to be funny, it just was.'

Harlene's non-appearance might have been written into

one of Woody's comedy routines, a typical situation from which any number of laughs would spring. But those who knew him doubt if she could have seen the funny side of it. Poor Harlene wasn't always on Woody's wavelength. She couldn't enjoy the more esoteric reaches of his behaviour. When she took wounded exception to his sallies about her, leading later to such distressing friction and court actions, she was demonstrating how little she understood the daemon of mirth driving this man she had married. To Christopher Hewett, the basic problem was that 'Harlene was everything Woody shouldn't have married.' That may be harsh, but would either of them deny it now?

Hewett agrees that the way Woody later used a parody of his marriage problems in his nightclub act 'really did slay her'. Yet he, and other friends, know that it was never his intention to hurt Harlene, or to belittle their marriage.

It was Harlene's misfortune that Woody's talent depended on a distorting ability to satirise only those experiences he personally felt and understood. Thus, his parents, his school, the whole of Brooklyn and what he had seen of California and the world, became targets for his bitterest wit. Not as expressions of real revulsion or dislike, but in mockery of truth in the way that great clowns have always mocked our real world. Indeed, as Woody's progenitors of humour showed time and time again, from the Samson of the *Old Testament* (who mocked even his closest relatives) to Charlie Chaplin's distillation of pathetic humour in poverty, the funny-bone is best tickled by devilish fingers.

Chris Hewett admits, 'I probably was evil enough to think that what Woody said about Harlene, or their marriage, in his routines was funny at the time. Because I thought, well, he's just getting it out of his system. I never thought of it as being malicious in any way.'

He has his own theory about Woody's and Harlene's joint problems. 'I'm sure she loved him,' he says, 'but I'm not at all sure he should ever have married. Or that he is the marrying kind. There are people who should not, ever, and he may be one of them. I don't know.' Then he adds, ruefully: 'I certainly am – as I discovered a long time ago when I was best man at the wedding of the girl I wanted to marry.'

Seeing the reaction of other women to Woody – 'they all loved him, everybody loved Woody' – Hewett still wonders where his special charisma sprang from. 'Woody was fascinating as a person and to work with but I always felt he was searching. And I never knew quite what it was for.'

Whatever it was – or, indeed, if it existed at all – Woody's 'search' would seem to have originated in boredom with a marriage which was failing to keep pace with his working environment, but from which he was too sensitive to break out. 'He'd never be unkind to anyone,' Hewett continues, 'I always think that if ever I had to go to work for Woody again as an actor he'd treat me like everybody else, in spite of my having directed him quite fiercely at times.

'He was the same to everyone in the company. If somebody's work did not come off – even if he was the failure of the week – Woody would always go out of his way to be extremely helpful in the most unselfish way. He'd do everything he knew, altering his script and so on, to try to make the thing work. And if it didn't, in the end, he wouldn't complain or lose faith. He'd just say "oh, well, it was worth a try."'

Christopher Hewett looks back over the years, shaking his head: 'One understands now,' he says, 'that life for him can't have been a bed of roses at the time. I mean, to have to work all day under the circumstances we worked under, and then at night to go back to the hut and play your recorder with a wife who was not ever, so far as I could see, in tune with him spiritually, must have been heavy going.'

Yet he, too, saw nothing to suggest that the final split between Woody and Harlene came through any dalliance on his part with the many attractive young women around, both in and out of the company. 'He had that little, snaky something called charm for them all,' he remembers, 'and not because he was then Woody Allen, because he had yet to make his name. He was just very attractive. Perhaps he brought out the mother in them, I don't know, but I'm pretty sure he could have had all the fun he wanted if he'd ever given the time to it.'

Instead of which, Woody kept hard at work. The 1,500 or so Tamiment crowd, determined to get every cent's worth out of their vacations, were insatiable for entertainment. The place ate up sketches, routines, scripts. 'It was an exhausting day for us,' Hewett agrees. 'First call was usually about ten. Then we'd all have breakfast together, maybe take a quick swim in the lake, then rehearse with a twenty-minute break for lunch until six. After that, if there wasn't a show, we'd probably set up a meeting with the writers or artists to discuss the next bill.'

As director, the slot he'd stepped into at short notice when the original director Moe Hack had hired dropped out (from fatigue?), Hewett was never free of commitment until the season ended. 'My own evenings were largely filled with preparing the next day's work,' he says. 'Remember, we were putting on a completely new show every Saturday night, and the whole of it had to be written and rehearsed during the week. That was where Woody was absolutely marvellous.

'As a writer, he could put the most bizarre things in the nicest possible way. On Wednesday nights he took part as a performer in the comedy sketches we put on, some of which he'd written and very often directed as well. Great stuff. He always wrote at least two sketches a week.'

'Yet somehow,' Hewett says, 'Woody did manage to enter into at least a few of the outdoor events and sports going on in abundance at the camp. Tennis, I think, and handball or volleyball were his favourites I remember. But he was a man who kept very largely to himself. And he was usually working, writing, so there wasn't much chance for anything else, certainly not for any capers.'

But not for lack of opportunity. The company were in a specially advantageous position. Hundreds of young, attractive girls and married women were in search of holiday fun. As the glamorous 'stars' of their live entertainments, even the writers and the members of the sixteen-piece orchestra could bank on a favourable reception to almost any proposition.

'The ladies found Woody fascinating, quite apart from those in the company,' Hewett recalls. 'It was his schoolboy charm. That terrific youthfulness he has, which every girl finds attractive. He was and is very Peter Pan-ish in a way. And I can see what they liked so much, those little oddities of his. Like Chaplin, and Chaplin was a great sex-fiend.'

Woody's appearance then, in his early twenties, was also less of a handicap than it had been. His hair was neater, the peak more pronounced and it was redder. But the one outstanding feature was the extraordinary appeal of those large, roving, often mischievous eyes. What Phil Berger calls their 'startled look, as if caught in an unspeakable act' tugged at every female heart. And Woody's kindness and shy sensitivity made women feel pleasantly understood. The problems only began when he went up on stage, as Chris Hewett found.

'He was very new to it,' he says. 'And not everyone thought he came across well. The trouble was he had such a quiet voice. We had to mike him up a lot and this wasn't always easy. It got in the way of action.'

Fred Ebb agrees: 'We all advised Woody against doing performances, and I don't recall him doing many after that. But there was a book show we wrote together where he played a cameraman and I was an advertising agent. He didn't have anything to say in the piece, but every time I looked over and saw him *shlepping* this enormous camera I couldn't stop laughing. It became almost impossible to get my lines out. It wasn't that he was hamming or trying to steal the scene, but the way he managed to screw up every action he made, getting into a tangle of wires and off-balance situations, was marvellously and unintentionally funny. I really don't know why.'

Hewett recalls another sketch Woody directed, about a General trying to get into a missile launching site at Cape Kennedy. His friend Len Maxwell played the General. 'Brilliant,' says Hewett, 'but only under Woody's direction. I tried to do it once and it was nothing like as good. Woody also played in that one, he took the part of one of two technicians.'

Chuckling still at the recollection of that scene, he adds: 'It was disaster! I only had to look to laugh. His expression – well, you know what his face does to you. And those glasses! But nothing elaborate, as an actor he was always economic. Very. That sketch brought the house down, largely because of how he just looked in it.'

Hewett ponders the imponderable. Why Woody rib-tickled every audience who saw him play that and a dozen other sketches which he had written only days before and directed with a minimum of rehearsal time.

'Could it be that the humour was a little more ethnic down there?' he queries. 'The audiences and the company were predominantly Jewish. After all, you don't play the same in Newcastle as in London. You adapt.

'It could be that Woody had gone too far towards an ethnic appeal when he finished with us, because it didn't go over so well with a wider audience. Not originally. When he started out in New York as a stand-up comic, I'd say he was a shade *too* ethnic, instead of just being himself. Which gave him great vulnerability.'

Ethnic, certainly, in Woody's side-busting original sketch about a massage parlour. Fred Ebb remembers that. Chris Hewett, though, believes it was set in a Manhattan cocktail party. Either way it was hilarious, and a model for later sight gags in his films and plays (often, to their private concern, featuring his parents.)

'Two lonely guys stumble into the "massage parlour",' Fred explains, making it obvious that the place was a thinly disguised if surrealist brothel, 'and one by one the girls are sent in to them for approval.

'But each one was got up to look like Groucho Marx! They all wore the same stuff: big, false, hooked nose, heavy black moustache and glasses with rolling eyes. Once again, this was tremendously funny. And once again I can't tell you *why* it was.'

Chris, who has kept a copy of the script, seems to be referring to the same sketch when he talks about it, but his recollection is of a social gathering in which all the guests looked like Groucho. 'It was one of the funniest things he ever did,' he says. 'As each guest arrived the laughs got bigger until the audience were in stitches. We all were.'

One of the actors at Tamiment in that final season of 1959 was Bob Dishy. This quiet, pipe-smoking stage humorist became a good friend to both Woody and Harlene. It was a friendship which continued when all three of them got back to New York at the end of the season. Dishy recalls another of Woody's sketches which won a lot of laughs from the camp audiences. It featured Doctor Albert Schweitzer.

The 'saint of the jungle' was then in the last years of his life, an object of reverence to most Americans. To Harlene, too, he was a man above men. But Woody's gentle mockery was totally inoffensive – and very funny, says Bob Dishy.

The theme of the piece was Schweitzer's secret passion to have a ventriloquist's dummy, which would answer inane questions for him. 'Lenny Maxwell played the old man,' Dishy recalls, 'and I was an associate. I'd come in with news of all the grave issues the world was involved in, and his doll would answer. It really worked extremely well. The audiences got it straight away.'

Alas, the same could hardly be said of the world outside. Woody's summer retreat had provided good years, even if the rewards were practically nil. The training it gave him in stage craft, the tremendous pressure from directing his own work and sometimes acting in it, as well as the solid professional attitude of everyone working with him down there at Tamiment, had been a valuable experience. In terms of lifelong assets, it had paid handsomely, whatever the cost to his marriage.

But time and Woody's career were moving along. As the pressures of his work increased, it seems that Harlene and he simply drifted apart. There was no noticeable, open conflict. She says now that for a year, they tried separation. no doubt as a trial of how each could manage. Yet all too palpably, these had been growing between them both.

For Woody it must have been a year of revelation. Freedom gave him the first real chance he had had to develop strict habits and concentrated work schedules. No longer was there the need to worry about another person's welfare, or to consider a partner's viewpoint or opinion. He was out on his own, ready for the big jump into full-scale performance.

The only questions were how to balance himself for the leap, and which of his developing skills to favour. Should it be writing for the theatre? Creating a more sophisticated comedy routine, based on Tamiment and the gags he had written for Garry Moore and others during the NBC years? Or his secret, most serious aim: the making of a film?

It shouldn't happen to a dog

The good news was that Woody's contract with Harvey Meltzer had run its course, and two of the world's most considerate and hardworking managers, Jack Rollins and Charles Joffe, had taken him up. Less promising was the uncertainty. Which way should he head?

'This was a hard time for Woody,' says Bob Dishy. 'He and Harlene and I had kept together after Tamiment when we were back in New York. I saw he was working things out in himself and seriously concerned about what to do. Then there was his marriage, of course.'

Woody's ambition, Bob felt, was and always had been to write. 'He was always well focused, if not a live wire. We'd go to movies and restaurants together, and it always had to be films and places to eat which Woody felt were really worthwhile. Not a waste of time. He took everything like that very seriously.'

Just occasionally, this led to what Bob Dishy thinks may have been embarrassing moments. He particularly remembers a night when the three of them went to a Chinese restaurant, one which Woody maintained would produce food in the way only the best Chinese gourmets understood it.

On their way there, Woody sounded enthusiastic. His aired knowledge of exactly what should, and should not, be done to create Chinese cuisine suggested an appreciation of oriental dishes which was impressive, according to Dishy. He himself took over the ordering, choosing with a precision which further emphasised his epicurean tastes, his friend says.

The waiter, having taken the order, disappeared. Woody relaxed. He seemed to be savouring the vision of his approaching feast. When it came, there were half a dozen small bowls and dishes filled with exotic succulence. Dishy remembers that he tasted each in turn before offering its contents to the others. 'Aha,' he said masterfully, 'the real thing!' Harlene looked – and Bob Dishy remembers feeling – deeply impressed. They took delicate helpings and began to eat.

Somewhere about their second mouthfuls Dishy remembers, the waiter hurried back to their table. Without a word, he says, the man brusquely collected up all the dishes and swept them away. 'Wrong order,' he said fiercely. 'This not for you. Yours coming now.'

It was a good moment, Dishy recalls, not to look too closely at Woody's embarrassed face. 'If the waiter had made the error, and not Woody,' he says now laughing. 'At least Woody had the grace to overlook it.'

Dishy saw no hint of Woody's marriage problem at that time. 'Harlene seemed to be getting along fine with him,' he remembers. 'But she was always a quiet type, and I never really knew what she was thinking. I can remember seeing her at Tamiment in the restaurant, and she was doing some kind of job, checking on the number of guests or tables I believe. I suppose she was working for Moe Hack at that time. I never got really close to her, and it was a surprise to me when I heard they'd got divorced, towards the end of '61 I think it was. I'd no idea what caused it, or if they'd separated already by then. But on reflection I guess she just didn't like showbusiness too much. That may have been a reason, because Woody's concentration was terrific.'

It needed to be. Breaking into the major ranks of America's New York-based writers is the professional equivalent of scaling the outside of the Empire State Building in slippers. It needed stamina, business ability and a bubbling, irrepressible fountain of wit and humour. For Woody to reach the peaks as he did (becoming one of America's highest paid writers, earning up to $1,700 in a week) was to take a rare combination of skills such as Rollins and Joffe could and did provide.

How Woody reached their consciousness is perhaps not the most momentous event in his ascent to world status. But, curiously, neither of the two managing impresarios have the complete story. Not even the true details of how he came to them, or what had been going on in his life before then.

Jack Rollins is a disarmingly nice man. With dark, heavy pouches under his eyes and near-black, greying hair sleeked and oiled, he could be type-cast as a Mississippi riverboat gambler of the Teddy Roosevelt era. One can see him in spats, a banded cigar rolling in his full lips. But the eyes lack any suggestion of flint. Rollins, one would say, is happiest (when not at the race-track, watching his own horse earn its feed) at home with his wife and family.

In fact a stranger knowing nothing of Rollins' role might sum him up as a comfortable, successful, middle-aged businessman. A little old-fashioned in dress and ways, and someone who has made good and is conscious of his debt to society and his clients. There is an aura of cautious geniality about him. Nothing aggressive. In his partnership with Joffe, all dealing is done by the latter. But in their association with Woody, it is unquestionably Rollins who made the marriage in the first place, his shy and pleasant personality responding naturally to Woody's introversion. It was Joffe's shrewd business abilities which forged a remarkable alloy from the three of them.

'Woody came to us in the first place because we were handling Mike Nichols and Elaine May (two well-known New York cabaret artistes). They were just starting and were almost unknown outside New York at that time.' Jack Rollins pauses to light the inevitable cigar which, in his round features, is a little unexpected – as is the twirled moustache of a stage villain.

'We had a small café, a room seating no more than fifty people. A temporary little place which disappeared after a year or so and, in fact, never made its mark. But, anyway, we were working. And Woody Allen came down to see the show.'

The cigar is wreathing silver trails of smoke into the air of the vast, high-ceilinged old office where Rollins, Joffe and occasionally Woody Allen and his tireless secretary Norma-Lee Clark spend innumerable hours. It is a curious sanctuary, more like a relic of Czarist Russia than the video and silicon-assisted space age outside. In the main 'salon', or reception office, hang two gigantic, mysterious paintings of jet-robed priests belonging to some Greek or Russian orthodoxy, set against voids of lime-green and holding what appears in one case to be a death's-head mask between aquiline hands. Elsewhere are Polynesian primitives and framed antique prints of trotting horses. But it is the room itself which explains these unlikely *objets d'art*.

It is part of a proud old building on Manhattan's 57th Street at number 130, a place of historic interest and a certain charm, though given to alarmingly slow, wheezing elevators which Woody is reputed to be terrified of. The reason, one suspects, for retaining this air of faded grandeur is part sentimentally and part devotion to pure *kitch*. An office is an office is an office. This is a home as well.

So Rollins, mastering an incipient middle-aged spread with difficulty, lounges on an overstuffed plum-coloured sofa set in an open rectangle facing a huge white fireplace where no fire glows. Under his feet, sharply protected by handmade, well-polished brown brogues – but lacking the dove-grey spats which would set him off to perfection – is a fine carpet in the shade of brown seen best in freshly-ground Kenya coffee; neither too light nor too sombre. The room is lit by enormously tall, studio-like windows at one end, towering perhaps twenty or so feet from floor to ceiling and equally wide. Tall, white, double doors connect through to the nerve-cell office which, under a lowered ceiling, contains the desks of Rollins and Joffe, and the working area of Norma-Lee.

She sits, looking competent and efficient, at her typewriter and battery of telephones. A small woman wearing lightly-framed spectacles, she is wearing red, a colour which accentuates her own softer shades of hair and complexion. There is about Norma-Lee, as about all secretaries and assistants of the great, the famous and the influential, an air of acolyte-like devotion.

Others serve at the same shrine. Rollins' daughter, a thin, nervous, dark-haired girl, is one of the staff. He announces it proudly. Two alert young whippets of Jewish youth run messages, use telephones, bring coffee, and appear as much at home in the incongruous opulence as on a film-set. Each looks as Woody may well have looked at their age, perhaps still in their teens. Perhaps they too are relatives (is a certain understandable nepotism the order of the day?).

There are other items in the salon, ornamenting its incongruity. A British award given to Charles Joffe in '79, for his production of *Manhattan*. It is a bronze mask with one eye closed in a wink. Also a silver figurine of a cat in a blue satin case, awarded for some television triumph.

Then there is a showcase full of various nuts . . . *Nuts*?! That's right. Also gourds, looking undusted and lifeless under the main coffee table. It is the one winking eye in the mask, one feels, which may have earned pride of place here – certainly if Woody had anything to do with this collection of art, souvenir and bric-a-brac.

Jack Rollins's dark eyes twinkle. The cigar glows. The subject of Woody, now that he's started on it, can only be of interest since it has taken this unlikely showman from the outer reaches of minor promotion and exploitation to the storm-centre of Entertainment's universe. Woody has carried them all with him, though the way Rollins and Joffe work for their artistes has undeniably contributed. Almost unique is the concentrated attention they give to every single performance, attending each and every act in person ('when we're not there, we're sick or dead,' says Rollins) and urging, cajoling, flattering and sometimes, but not often, criticising.

No doubt about it, Rollins can take his bow on the same stage as Woody and Charles Joffe any night of the week. The fact that he very seldom does is a tribute to his personal modesty. It does nothing to diminish what this showman has accomplished.

'Woody came to see me that night,' he says. 'He asked if we could conceivably be interested in him as a writer of material for our artistes.'

Jack Rollins's eyes look seriously pained. 'The answer,' he says slowly, 'was no. Because there was no need for any of the artistes we represented to use his or anyone else's material. They didn't need it.'

If that no had been final, the whole axis of Woody Allen, superstar, would have shifted. He would have found other markets and other managements to buy his material and represent him. They, Jack and Charley, might have stayed with little-known artistes and small, try-out cafés. All that is conjecture, but it prompts the question which Rollins is slow to answer: 'Would you have taken Woody on if you'd known how successful he was going to be?'

'Well,' he says finally, 'you do what you can.'

His entire philosophy lies in the words. To Jack Rollins, the high-flying, ulcerating escalation of his business, lifting him to producer credits and personal involvement in Woody's films, plays, writings and appearances, has forced a series of increasing pressures such as he may never have invited or intended. For his partner, Joffe, it was probably a different story, but one sees in Rollins a man who could have been comfortable with far less. Nevertheless, as he says, 'you do what you can'. And that is what he did, from the day he and Charles Joffe accepted Woody as a client.

'I didn't see Woody for three, maybe four, months after that night,' he says. 'Then he came back and asked if we would consider handling him as his managers. He was a writer, for television, and normally we didn't handle writers *per se*. We handled, and still do, performers who may also write. If that's what they do, then we handle their product.'

So why take on this little-known, less than prepossessing young writer who claimed to have no experience or ambition in performing?

'Why did we? Because there was simply an indefinable

thing about him. We looked at his material, of course, and to us it was incredibly funny. But our reason for taking him on went beyond the material. It was something about *him*, something you can't put your finger on.

'He'd waltz in with that bony nose and serious mien and we'd break up and laugh. Aside from his writing, we both thought this guy hilariously funny.'

Still reflecting on the mystery of the talent which has made his fortune, Jack Rollins draws gently on the remains of his cigar. The eyes are pensive, seeking an explanation. There isn't one apparently. 'Now you've got to remember this is the shyest man I've ever met,' he says. 'To this day. *Truly* shy. And we've had him with us now for more than fifteen years (actually twenty). What is he now, forty-one? (Woody was forty-five at the time). Well, I don't know what it was made him so funny to us, but I'd guess it was partially because of his inordinate shyness.'

It was the quality which had stamped him all through. At school. With family and friends. With girls. Even in Tamiment, when he wasn't up to his eyes in work. It was behind Max Liebman's refusal to accept that he *could* speak in public. And Bob Dishy's understanding of the agony any embarrassment could cause him. It was the reason why at Midwood he had participated in none of the activities, or earned more than passing indifference from Barbara Lieberman.

It was also the obstacle to his performing, other than in out-of-the-way sites like Tamiment, on the public stage. It stood forcibly in the path of Jack and Charley's instinctive urge to see Woody put over his own material in his own way.

'Woody was a guy who lived purely by his intellect, his brain,' Jack says. 'He would go into his room, shut out the world and write jokes which he'd conceived in his mind. But getting him to express these was like asking a piano to speak. Even on a personal basis, you know, he found communicating difficult.'

So when Jack and Charley suggested he move into the

role of stand-up comic, performing his own material, Woody, as Jack remembers, 'was surprised, if not a little shocked', by the idea. He said only that he'd like to think about it, Jack says. 'He didn't like coming out in the open. Not at all. But I'll tell you that this guy has the guts and courage of a second-storey man. And the self-discipline he has I've never seen in any other human being.'

It took all of three weeks for Woody to nerve himself, nevertheless. And probably nobody but Jack Rollins could have persuaded him to make the vital decision. 'I could always get to him,' Jack admits. 'I guess this was the thing that kept us together. Both Charley and I are very close, always have been, and we work as a team.'

It is a team which has handled many gifted people: Harry Belafonte, Mike Nichols and Elaine May and a whole star-roster of others who are, in Jack's view, 'pretty terrific'. The difference with Woody was that he called for every ounce of their personal backing and encouragement, none of which could be faked. 'Let me put it like this,' Jack says. 'Anybody that shy can't really enjoy putting himself on display. On the stage, in a role, an actor is playing a character. But down there in the café he has to be himself. That is a very difficult thing to accomplish. Unpleasantly difficult.'

When Woody came in and announced his decision, he made it clear he had no great confidence in what they believed he could do. They'd told him they thought they'd glimpsed something in him, a unique quality. But he wasn't nearly so sure. They had only seen him going over his written material, to judge its effect on them. Whatever it was they thought he had was unknown to him. He was the last person to recognise it in himself.

'I'd like to try it,' he told his managers, 'but you guys had better be ready to catch me when I fall.'

They were. 'We are always present when our artistes are performing,' Jack says. 'We've made it a practice in our business. It's where management ought to be. We have a very small number of artistes and give them total concentration and attention. Because only by that is a manager working and contributing. He shouldn't be an agent. He must travel with them, work with them, and be there every time they go on. I tell you, if we're not there it's because we're having a night off. So Woody knew we'd be out front watching his act, helping him shape and develop it. He had that amount of confidence in us by then, or he would never have done it.'

Jack says they put him into one of the smallest of their small cafés, in New York's Greenwich Village. Crowded cabaret clubs, mostly in dank basements or fly-blown attics. A packed crowd has paid entrance money and expects entertainment. It is massed under a small platform stage surrounded by black, bare walls. There is, with any luck, a piano alongside whose stained, ivory notes just about work. Some of the cafés are dry, selling only ice-cream and Coke. In Woody's day, this was normal.

His first appearance was at a two-stage cabaret called the Duplex on Grove Street. Nowadays, there's a grand piano in the minute room on the upper floor. Downstairs, music flows over a larger crowd ranked in curving lines round the stage. Anything other than rock music would be drowned in the hum and bustle of chatter and shuffling feet. Anyone with as low a profile and as weak a voice as Woody would pass practically unnoticed.

And for a gruelling, exhausting and near-suicidal year and a half, this is what happened to him at the Duplex and elsewhere. Ironically, one of his first appearances was at The Bitter End.

'To start with, he was terrible,' Jack Rollins admits, 'He was *terrible*. Perhaps the worst comedian you've ever seen, literally.'

He and Charley suffered with him, as they did with all their artistes. In the eyes of experienced showman, Max Gordon, who ran the Village Vanguard, one of the biggest, busiest and most successful of the club-theatres, Jack Rollins was 'crazy about Woody, to the point where nothing would stop him persevering with what might have seemed to anyone else a hopeless task'.

Max sees it with the professional eye of a seasoned New

York impresario. His words on the subject, emerging from a bullet-shaped head in which the mouth is hardly ever without its clamped cigar (even at nine o'clock in the morning when its owner is working in pyjamas in his Fifth Avenue apartment), spare no one. But he remembers Jack's agony all too clearly.

'I've written it all down in my book,' he says, 'just as it happened, though I used a fictional device there (*Live at The Village Vanguard*, St Martin's Press, 1980). Let me tell you Jack was in a real state about this new act he'd added to his stable, and when Herb Jacobi and I came into the Blue Angel one night he was really keen for us to meet this Woody Allen. I guess nobody'd heard of him at that time.'

Those who had were more likely saying things about the act which would have stung Woody's ears and given Jack and Charley sleepless nights, if they weren't suffering them already. As Max Gordon says: 'I didn't know he'd been on stage. We came down and shook hands with Jack. He had this kid with him, wearing big glasses under a mop of untidy hair. He was the only one at the table, so it had to be this Woody. But to me he looked like just a short, frightened kid.'

When Jack introduced them, Max's impression became even stronger. 'The kid had a weak kind of handshake, as if he was too shy to get close to you,' he says. 'Anyway, we all sat down. And Jack said to me, "You've got to believe this is the most brilliant writer of comedy material in the business. But what this kid does is give it away! He doesn't do what other comedians are making a fortune out of doing – getting up on stage and performing his work. He just lets it go for virtually peanuts!"'

Max chuckles. 'I remember Jack pointed down at Woody's feet which weren't too well shod at the time. He said, "You see, he walks all over New York with his toes sticking out of his shoes, while the guys he's writing for are driving their Cadillacs!" Jack was getting really worked up, which for him was extraordinary. But I could see he and Woody got along pretty well, because the kid was sitting there drinking it all in as if his father was talking to him.

'So Jack turns to him and says: "Haven't I told this to you a hundred times? If only you'd get up and do the material yourself, you could be rich. Instead of which *you* are the *schlep* walking around town like a tramp, and they make it good on your stuff." I watched the kid when he said this, and honest to God he didn't show anything. Not even anger. He just looked up like somebody'd told him he was a great writer, and would he autograph one of their books!'

Max shakes his head like a pocket-sized Napoleon, which he closely resembles. 'Jack kept pounding into him,' he says. 'Telling him all he needed to do was to just get up on his hind legs on stage. "All you need is a mid-Manhattan showcase," he said. "You need the Blue Angel which Max here and Herb Jacobi are running. They'll give you a break." He turned to me: "Won't you do that for me' Max? I tell you, this kid is really good. You won't regret it."

'I looked at Herb and he looked at me. We were both doubtful. But Jack was a good manager. That much we knew. And he'd done us quite a few good turns, bringing us people like Harry Belafonte and Mike and Elaine.

'We didn't especially need anyone, though. We had plenty of good people we could call on in those days. Everyone knew us and the place, and there was no shortage of talent wanting to work the Blue Angel. As Jack said, it was a wonderful showcase.'

So Max Gordon and his partner hesitated. Maybe Jack was right again? He had never picked a wrong one yet. Or maybe he'd landed himself with a writer who couldn't act, however much he tried to force him into it? Obviously a manager makes more profit from a performer than he does from a writer, because a stand-up comic with first-class material and a following can make twenty times what a writer gets paid for his work.

'We had to take that into account as well,' Max agrees. 'But Jack was very persuasive. "Salary doesn't matter," he said. "Pay Woody what you like. But give him a chance to prove what I say. And don't take him off until he's done it. I want him to have a good run and you can have any contract you like, with options. So if he comes up trumps you can hang on to him. How about that?''

'I still held back. Jack spread his hands wide. "Look," he said. "If he loses money for you I'll pay his salary myself!"

'I took that as something of a figure of speech because, although I knew Jack wasn't short of a few dollars, I couldn't see him ever paying one of his artistes out of his own pocket. But, anyway it made me smile. And, since it was Jack, and Herb and I both owed him something, I nodded agreement. I'd give him a chance, I said. Looking at Woody, which I did, I couldn't tell whether he was pleased or not. He still looked what he was I guess, terrified.'

What Max Gordon paid Woody Allen for that early booking is forgotten. It was certainly no great amount. Probably, in the nature of things at that time and in that place, around $100 a week. It could have been a little more, and it may well have been considerably less in view of Jack's heavy selling of the product.

In his book, Max says he uses a fair amount of showman's licence in recounting this story of Woody's early performing days. But it seems to ring true. He also fictionalises, or as he puts it 'semi-fictionalises', an account of Jack's problems once Woody had made his first disastrous appearances and been given a largely indifferent reception by Blue Angel audiences.

'I can't remember exactly,' he says, 'but it's true that the kid was scared, still scared.' In Max's eyes Woody was also a dubious talent as an entertainer. But he was at least inexpensive. 'We weren't paying him the kind of money that hurt, so we let him run. All in all, he was with us three months. And he was learning, there's no doubt about that. He was really putting himself out to pick up everything he could.'

Woody was doing this from Max, from Jack Rollins, and from anybody else who knew their business. 'But it was Jack,' says Max, 'who kept hammering at him not to give it all up. Otherwise I feel sure he'd have thrown in the towel before he was half way through the engagement.

'He was taking a lot of punishment. Only the real high-brow people, the sophisticated few enjoyed or understood his low-key delivery and style: what I call the "*shlemiel* approach". For the rest he was a nothing.'

A nothing who was beginning to believe in his own lack of ability, that was the problem. Jack Rollins sensed it. 'He used to stand at the back every night,' Max recalls. 'He didn't miss a word of Woody's show, and he couldn't believe the lack of appreciation he was getting down there. One night he called me over during the intermission and asked me into Woody's dressing room to try to give a little encouragement, which he badly needed.

'I'd heard Jack shouting in there, telling Woody he was doing all right. To me he said: "Max, *please* tell him he's doing okay." The kid wouldn't listen to him. He was sitting there with his hands over his ears. "Max, tell him," Jack begged me. "Tell Woody he's not terrible. He thinks he's terrible." Then he swung round and patted Woody's shoulder. "You're doing terrific. You hear? Terrific!" Then he said to me, in a whisper. "Tell him, Max. Tell him how terrific he's doing!" '

Which for Max Gordon wasn't easy. Woody had played the Duplex, where the audience was less hard to please, and where the relationship between stage and the packed-in group was more intimate, less like a theatre. Here at the mid-town Blue Angel and at the Bitter End, which he also played occasionally, he was failing, night after night.

Dick Roffman, seasoned journalist and New York PR specialist remembers how he watched Woody Allen's performance around that time. It must have been one of Woody's earliest mid-town Manhattan appearances, on a night when Roffman was prowling around backstage waiting for one of his celebrity clients to finish dressing. Woody was about to go on.

'This was a smart nightclub, the sort of place up on the West Side which attracted an educated crowd. Woody was pacing up and down. At first I thought he was nervous, which was understandable. Then I realised he was doing what a lot of artistes do before they go on, he was *willing* himself to hit the right note. As I watched, he seemed to me to gain confidence all on his own, the closer he got to going on.

'It stuck in my mind because nearly everyone else I'd ever seen perform, certainly when they were new to the business, did pretty much the opposite. They got *more* nervous, not less, the closer they came to their act. Woody was actually enjoying the thrill of using his own material, I believe. Savouring it. And he loved it!'

If he did, it was a masochistic kind of love. Woody, according to Jack Rollins, was dying a thousand deaths on most stages he played on. His lack of nervousness may have been a genuine act of will, and of knowing he was ready with his own script in his head to go on. But it was the courage of the gladiator not of any showbusiness Caesar.

Another Woody-watcher who spotted him backstage at the Blue Angel in those perilous early try-outs was Gary Stevens, a syndicated newspaper columnist. Gary felt sorry for the man he saw pacing up and down behind the scenes. As he says, 'Woody was like a cat on hot bricks.' Stevens went up to Woody, intending to offer a few words of cheer. 'I remember I said something like, "Don't worry, Woody, everyone who has real talent feels scared before they go on." And he looked at me with that funny look of his and said, "Oh I'm not nervous. It's just that I want to go to the bathroom. And I'm not sure there'll be time."'

Gary Stevens had seen Woody at the Vanguard and watched the way the crowd reacted. 'It was actually kind of mixed,' he says. 'There were people who thought he was uproarious. Others found him totally unfunny. They were just completely outside his range.'

It was a range that Jack and Charley were striving to expand. But it was a terribly hard task. Woody was fatalistically appearing, night after night, with as little hope of the sort of success they dreamed of as of being the next president of the USA.

Do him something

Woody's act was so low-key that an audience had to listen; to pay attention. And to know that, however dumb he sounded, or shy and nervous he seemed, this was all part of it. The humour came out of the *persona* he was creating: entangling himself in the microphone cord as if unused to any such instrument, wearing the clothes of a scene-shifter. All this was integral to the image. You had to know that, and concentrate, or he became meaningless.

To Phil Berger 'the *futzing* around Allen did on stage was the *gestalt* of a comic anti-hero. The elliptical pauses, the scratching, the hesitant voice: true neurotica.' Which is another way of saying that he was deliberately portraying that *nebbish* quality which so many others, including his old schoolteachers, had mistaken for the real Woody.

The neuroses, however, were genuine. Insoluble marriage problems and approaching divorce seemed to inflame them. He began regular treatments of psychoanalysis at this time, and has never been without them since. He was, as Rollins noted: 'Deeply troubled, but the most uncomplaining guy in the world. His neuroses, and God knows he's neurotic, are the only outward signs of problems he'll never place on any other human being's shoulders.'

Nevertheless, however much of a stoic he was, Woody must have begun to wonder if it could be worth the agony. His is an individual style: either an audience gets the point, or his act is likely to baffle them. Nothing he could do would alter that fact. Yet, financially and creatively there was no reason, other than an indomitable reluctance to give up, why he should not quit.

95

He was writing for the Garry Moore show, which earned the rent for the apartments he briefly inhabited on the outer fringes of fashionable Manhattan. Though still unknown outside the profession, he had collected one of television's many accolades in winning a Sylvania award for his work on the Sid Caesar show. Also, in company with many other promising young writers, he had received nominations for an Emmy. Now that he was a regular writer for several of television's top names, Herb Shriner, Art Carney, Kaye Ballard, Carol Channing, Pat Boone, he could live comfortably and well. It was a far easier life than performing.

As celebrity interviewer Lee Guthrie noted: 'He still shudders when forced to recall those days leaving a nice, safe, warm typewriter to go out into the freezing cold and stand on a bare stage and make a fool of himself.' Or as she quotes him saying: 'It was unspeakably agonising. I didn't know what I was doing. All day long, I would shake and tremble thinking about standing up that night before people and trying to be funny.'

The year Woody worked at the Duplex was, he said, 'the worst of my life. I'd feel this fear in my stomach the minute I woke up, and it would be there until I went on at 11 o'clock at night. I'd have a sensation of relief after I finished the second show but the next morning it would start all over again.'

It got so bad that his work suffered. Garry Moore dropped him. 'I was fired from the show, and didn't blame them,' he said later. 'But after that I wasn't making a cent.'

And the way things were going with Harlene made things even worse. One day it all came to a head. At three in the morning when he'd finished working, he saw Jack Rollins. 'Look,' he said, 'I think I've tried it long enough.'

Jack sees that moment as the single most influential flux in the forging of Woody Allen's career under his and Charley's management. To explain why, he returns to the anomaly of Woody, established as a writer capable of earning several hundred dollars a week, working his head off for peanuts. 'He wasn't even getting his cab fare,' he says.

'Night after night he was going out there for maybe thirty minutes. There was no contact. He wasn't getting to them because he couldn't, he didn't know how. He looked weird and funny, but there was no contact.'

The astonishing thing is that Jack recognised all this yet still believed, doggedly, in making it work. 'I remember saying to him, "Woody, you can become a performer. I know you can. And at a very good level."

'That's what I believed then, and always had believed in spite of the fact that he had worked eighteen months without getting anything like the success I saw as his due. And Charley backed me up. We both explained that he was a hothouse comic, not a natural. He had to be cultivated into it, like a rare plant. Where most natural performers had spent the first ten years of their lives, even as kids, thinking and working towards live performances, his background was the opposite. He had to force himself – and against one of the shyest natures I've ever known or ever will.'

So Rollins told him, 'Look, give it one more try. I know it's easy for me to say this, but I do believe you can do it. Even if it's only an opinion, don't throw it away before you give it one last chance.'

He recalls how Woody looked at him, doubt and tiredness in his eyes. 'I'll think about it,' was all he said. For two days Jack and Charley didn't know if they still had a performer named Woody Allen on their books, or only a writer.

'Then he came to us,' Rollins says. 'I'd left the decision to him because he was the one taking the beating every night, not us. It had to be Woody's last shot, if it was going to work. And he had to *want* to do it.'

He was banking, too, on the extraordinary steel inside Woody which treated all opposition, even the indifference of his nightclub audiences, as a challenge rather than a put-down. And finally he was rewarded.

'Woody told us, "If you fellas think I haven't given it enough time, and that I still have the potential to be a performer, then I'm going to try it a bit longer. I'll give it another month." '

As Jack Rollins says: 'That was it. We knew he meant it. Amazingly in that month it really began to take shape. Not at any one particular moment but slowly, over a period, things began to change. And Woody started to relax. You know, I'd say that it was that final decision he made to give it just one more month which made him work differently, more successfully. He knew, now, that if it went on as badly as before he only had those final four weeks to last out. So he stopped worrying so much.'

Maybe, too, the decision Woody had taken kept Harlene's disapproval at bay. Jack Rollins saw how opposed she was to Woody's nightly exposures to failure. 'She was there with him during all this very difficult time, all that first year,' he explains, 'and my impression was that she felt we were misdirecting him. In fact one night she came to us and asked, "What are you trying to do to him?"'

What they were trying to do was to urge, cajole and persuade Woody to reveal a talent for making people laugh which at that time hid behind a barricade of shyness and self-effacement. Harlene, Jack noted, did not see things as Woody saw them. 'She was trying to help him,' he says, 'but not along the way he was developing.'

Which, of course, was the way Jack and Charley, with Woody's reluctant but determined compliance, had set him on. 'I didn't know Harlene very well,' Jack reflects, 'but I'd say she would have felt a lot happier if he could have been a doctor or a lawyer rather than a monkey of a performer.

'She really felt we were mis-shaping him. I got the feeling that she had come from a nice, respectable, bourgeois background and just didn't like what we were doing to her husband. The intellectual side of it – his writing and so on – that was OK. But the showbusiness end, that was something she found distasteful.'

He makes this admission with no show of regret. If Harlene failed to see what he and his partner saw and clung to in their strangely diffident client, and if her marriage foundered at this difficult time partly as a result, then that, in the light of Woody's future success, is nothing to be ashamed of.

'Because we had faith in this man,' he says. 'We always thought our instinct about Woody was correct. We backed our judgement. And the change came, as I say, just in time.'

Not at one particular moment, Jack insists. But there was an evening of great importance, an evening he links in his memory to many others when major producers and impresarios would be persuaded to venture into the downtown clubs and cabarets where Woody was tying himself in knots, half strangling himself out of assumed or real nervousness with the mike cord, in vain attempts to bring laughter bubbling out of audiences so dead that he sometimes told them so.

Once, as Dick Cavett, one of the few early admirers of any importance he had attracted – and completely enslaved – recalls, Woody stopped his act to tell them to their faces that they were the worst audience he had ever seen or played to anywhere. He personally labelled them candidates for the *Guinness Book of Records*. But as they were chatting among themselves ordering food and drinks while he berated them in his habitual soft tones, few even heard what he had to say.

Fortunately Cavett was *not* the only perceptive viewer. There was one other, on this particular fruitful evening. As Jack was out in California at the time, it is natural that he should fail to see it now as the massive turning point for Woody which it became. The first Rollins knew about it, in fact, was when his partner Charles Joffe called him. 'By the way,' Charley told him across 3,000 miles of telephone cable. 'We had a strange character in today who works for Charles K. Feldman. What do you know? He *likes* Woody Allen.'

Feldman, producer of such smash Hollywood film hits as *The Seven Year Itch, A Streetcar Named Desire, The Glass Menagerie,* and *The Group* was a man with the golden touch. His nickname, the 'King Midas of Celluloid', had been earned by solid success. It was, for Woody, a fabulous opportunity, as Charley Joffe's visitor explained.

Sam Shaw was not what he looked, on that first visit to

the much smaller Rollins-Joffe office they then occupied, several doors from their present one. 'He came in to see Charley, wearing a sweater and sneakers,' Rollins explains. 'And in those days people didn't wear them on business visits. He also had a dirty old copy of the *New York Times* under his arm. If he was Woody's Good Fairy, he was the most unlikely looking one Charley had ever seen.'

Yet that's what he turned out to be. Because not only did Sam Shaw work as a photographer for Feldman, he was also a highly respected, popular figure with many Hollywood stars and directors in spite of his sartorial defects. Nor had he been alone in seeing Woody. He'd taken Shirley MacLaine with him to the Blue Angel and both had fallen in love with Woody from the moment he walked on stage.

'Sam, who is one of those wonderful people in the world and now a great friend of ours, had really taken to Woody,' Jack says. 'He thought he was brilliant. Every one of Woody's jokes scored with him. And he'd come to see Charley to talk business, because Feldman was working on an idea for a new movie and wanted a young, budding writer who hadn't worked for films before. So Sam was there to arrange for Charles Feldman to come and see Woody that same night.'

Even so, Jack, in California, didn't fall off his chair at the news. 'Because I knew some people were beginning to go for Woody,' he says, 'but not all. Still today, there are people who either love him or he doesn't move them at all. They either go crazy for him or they're kind of bewildered. They ask afterwards "What was that all about?" He may be getting to more and more people these days – in fact, it's really extraordinary, it's like ripples – but both those who like him and those who don't are equally strong in their views, and equally verbal about them.'

Would Feldman like him? That was the doubt in Jack's mind. Maybe he would, maybe he wouldn't. Woody was beginning to be noticed. He was also learning to use more technique, to reach out to people with his strange, low-key humour. But not everyone had the ear for what was basically New York, urban-Jewish wit based on personal experience and suffering. There are students of Woody and Chaplin, and other Jewish comics like Eddie Cantor and Groucho Marx, who believe that a Jew makes others laugh when he himself is weeping inside. It is a paradox of Jewish refusal to accept life, or one's lot in it, as anything but illusory and impermanent. If Feldman wanted that brand of funniness in his script, then Woody Allen was his man.

Happily, he did. The film the great producer had in mind was already written, as a vehicle for Warren Beatty. Feldman didn't like the script as it stood, but he liked the title. It had come to him in a flash of inspiration while Beatty was staying with him and calling up innumerable lady friends. Every time he lifted the receiver and heard one or the other of them purring on the end of the line, Beatty would ask 'What's new, pussycat?'

That, Feldman decided, was just the title he needed for his bawdy farce in which an irresistible young man with a low resistance to attractive female advances tries, with only moderate success, to cling to the straight and narrow.

It was a neat idea. But writing such an improbable script was so tongue-in-cheek that those who had already attempted it had not, in Charles Feldman's view, done sufficient justice to his theme. He needed somebody entirely fresh and different. In Woody, he could not have found anyone more fitted to the role.

So, to Jack and Charley's well-concealed delight, a deal was worked out. Woody has been reported as saying they offered him a 'tremendous amount of money'. Guthrie says he was paid $35,000, but 'Feldman was prepared to pay $60,000.' Perhaps for once in their managerial lives Jack and Charley had undersold a client. But as Feldman had been a Hollywood agent in his time, handling money-spinners like the Great Garbo, Marilyn Monroe and John Wayne, he was obviously a hard man to beat down, or up.

Aside from the terms, this was Woody's most transcending opportunity. Feldman saw him, liked him, and bought him. The following day he not only told Jack and Charley that they'd got a deal, but offered Woody a speaking part as well. In doing so he may have rewarded Rollins for all the hard work and heartache of the past eighteen months, but he also gave himself a subtle lever to control Woody's creative enthusiasm.

Whenever Feldman wanted to get the maximum out of Woody, say for some scene which had to be re-written for the n-th time, he'd just tell him: 'Write the thing for yourself.' It never failed, though most of the stuff Woody put in, where he had the best of the scene, was later reduced or cut out entirely.

It was only one trick in many. Woody had known film people. Some of the writers at Tamiment, and television stars he'd worked with, had had Hollywood experience. His own passage through the film capital had given him a chastening appreciation of the layer upon layer of falsity and ego-massage indulged in almost habitually in making movies. So he was not in the least naive about what he was doing.

The difference here was that he was up against a skilful, wily manipulator of talents. Feldman was a producer who acted as puppeteer. He searched endlessly for the new, the different, the budding geniuses of showbusiness. So he had acquired for *Pussycat* an as yet unknown composer, Burt Bacharach, to write the title number. Also a little known Welsh heartthrob singer named Tom Jones to sing it into women's hearts all over the world. And an English director, Clive Donner, who was little known outside BBC television. But he did not, as Woody was to complain feelingly, leave them alone to get on with it.

Still, the challenge was there, the money was good, and what Feldman paid for he usually got – as Woody found out. He has said it a hundred times since: 'He wanted a sex-sex girl-girl picture to make a fortune. I had something else in mind. What he got was a sex-sex girl-girl picture which made a fortune.' And, if Woody was unhappy with that – a film which nobody of permissive age could possibly mistake for a work of art, or taste – at least he could see some signs that his nightclub hair-shirt was beginning to pay dividends.

In the fading months of 1963 he was still at the Blue Angel, while working in the daytime on the *Pussycat* script. But already he was attracting laudatory attention.

In January that year he got a favourable notice from a girl reporter, Mary Pangalos. That was soon after opening at the Bitter End. 'Success,' she wrote 'has already altered his life somewhat.' It was followed by many more, increasingly favourable impressions of his emerging style as the inveterate 'loser', the little guy always being robbed and beaten up. Afraid of the dark, disliking animals and children and totally unable to fix anything about the house, he endeared himself to many who, secretly, had the same problems.

Indeed, the image had appeal if not charisma. Woody was appearing weekly on the Merv Griffiths television show and had personal appearances arranged for him at the curiously named 'hungry i' in San Francisco, at 'Mr Kelly's' in Chicago – where he was to meet his long-time friend, Jean Doumanian – and at the Village Gate. As Rollins had predicted, his talent as a performer was finally catching up.

It was at the last of these, the Gate, that *Time* magazine bestowed its accolade. In February 1963, Woody was given a notice which not only mentioned that his weekly paycheque had gone up from zero to $1,000, but also that 'he is not only an interesting new comedian but a rare one . . . he never mentions John F. Kennedy.'

In May, *Horizon* reported him as having moved to better quarters on New York's Upper East Side. By then he'd appeared, the magazine said, on several leading TV shows. On these, and in his act, he now joked repeatedly about the failure of his marriage. He had, he quipped, sold the memoirs of his love life to a toy-manufacturer who was going to make it into a game. Harlene had retired from the fray, powerless to counter – or avoid – reports of Woody's increasingly popular gags at her expense.

'The funniest monologist in town,' as the *New York Post* called him, was not above tossing in a few seemingly wry comments about his personal life. Columnist Gary Stevens believes his marriage to Harlene (and subsequently to actress Louise Lasser) broke up because 'the girls couldn't measure up to his fantasies. He's too concerned with himself – too spaced out – to be any girl's ideal mate.' Stevens adds despairingly: 'If you ask me, is he the marrying kind?, I'd have to say I hope not. For the sake of the women he might marry.'

The woman he had married, and stayed with for five years including their try-out separation, was finding his constant jibes at their marriage for the sake of his performance hard to live with. Though she later took Woody to court in a bitter series of two actions for defamation, she says now that she has no wish to harm him. 'We were happy together, I don't want any scandal,' she insists.

But friends saw her taking punishment she had no equipment to counter. Jack Rollins saw 'no noticeable sense of humour' in Harlene. Mickey Rose believes the ordeal Woody went through to get started as a performer contributed largely. 'It was a nerve-wracking time for him,' he says. 'Without Rollins and Joffe in there with him, watching him, every night, he'd never have done it.' Significantly, Rose makes no mention of Harlene. Presumably he did not see her as supporting him to any major degree.

In his eyes, the marriage could even have been a handicap. 'It's a *big* thing he was doing,' he says. 'I did it myself. Once a year only, for two years, so as to get rid of the fantasy. But I couldn't stand the life, and I don't know how Woody did.'

It involved physical as well as mental hardship, he says. 'All that going home at two a.m. (at weekends the Blue Angel floor show finished after one in the morning) on a wet, cold night. Or flying all over the country.' Woody, he says, has managed to get used to flying 'for all his reported neuroses'. Mickey Rose never did.

It was also a time when many of today's major stars were treading the same exhausting path up the same unyielding mountain. Rose says competition was fierce. 'People like Mike Wallace and Barbra Streisand were just getting on their feet,' he says. 'Woody knew Barbra. She lived over

Oscar's Fish Restaurant on Third Avenue, and they used to meet during that time when he was forcing himself to go on, and when fish was about the only food he could stomach.'

Bob Dishy, another friend who admired Woody's guts for sticking to his performances, also mentions only Jack and Charley as his main supporters. But as Dishy says: 'In Woody's personal life there must have been times when he became very depressed, but to my knowledge this never affected his work. He had enough discipline to overcome it.'

Dishy was with him the night Feldman and Shirley Mac-Laine watched Woody's act together. Woody knew they were there. He also knew, from what Charley Joffe had said, that something big was in the wind. 'I could see that Feldman really liked his act,' Dishy recalls, 'but Woody was nervous as a kitten. That Saturday we went to a movie and he couldn't sit still. He was waiting for a call which hadn't come and he was beginning to get the jitters.'

When the call did come, and Feldman sent over a script of *Pussycat* for Woody to look at, he said later he would like to have sent it back unread 'as I always did with scripts sent to me'. But loyalty to Rollins and Joffe made him take on the assignment. He knew it was going to involve him in a task where his own style would be utterly submerged. As he has said: 'If I could have had my way, it would have been a much better film, and lost money.' Feldman had no intention of letting that fate overtake him.

Pussycat made an estimated seventeen million dollars at the world's box-offices, benefitting everyone concerned. Peter O'Toole, who played the part Feldman had scheduled for Warren Beatty (and, according to some reports, Cary Grant earlier still) was notched even higher on the star ladder. Woody did his best to write himself into prominence but was systematically reduced in Feldman's cutting-room. He lacked any editorial control which could in his view have improved the script.

The paradox was that he apparently felt abused in having worked on the subject, yet it unquestionably guaranteed

105

his future backing in Hollywood. A contract to make his own pictures, in his own way and with no interference, followed from United Artists.

And yet, in a curiously ambivalent way, the film may not have been necessary to him. The critics and the audiences were waking up to his extraordinary humour. Newspaper columnists flocked now to interview him, struggling to portray this strange, funny guy as he really was. Dissecting Woody in print was becoming established as a top city sport in New York. And, with the national magazines showing their interest, he could have been all set for a career as a comic of Danny Kaye proportions. Maybe this would have happened had he never said a line in Feldman's block-buster.

'Bespectacled and milquetoastish,' critic Martin Burden called him. And 'spokesman of the fumble-fingered'. 'His rapport with audiences has been phenomenal,' wrote Joanne Stang. 'Sometimes troubled souls seek him out after performances to tell him that they have similar problems.'

Something else was noticeable in those early encounters with a fascinated, wholly gullible media. Woody was beginning to invent a public image for himself. What he told them, sometimes in obvious mockery, was a reflection of his emergence from the Brooklyn chrysalis. But it is clear from a careful reading of those press interviews that he was blending the remembered with the imagined in his past.

The distinction, which few could draw, lay between what he said in all seriousness and what he pulled inter-viewers' legs with as the professional clown he was. The blend lay in his head, the key to it often subtly disguised. Woody had put together a satirical second-self, a whimsical Doppelganger; for his own protection, it seems. And one wonders if even he knew, on occasion, which of the two he was parading. Since he claims to tell the truth in interviews – by which he no doubt means serious interviews – he must have found a more reliable way to discriminate than have most of his interrogators.

In December '63 he told Helen Dudar, *Post* special writer, about his early life in Flatbush. 'It was hectic,' she reported his saying. 'Partly because of economic circumstances, partly because of war-time apartment shortage. My family was always getting billeted with relations. There were uncles and cousins running in and out of rooms, and we were always moving.' This may well have been the truth.

He added that this may have accounted for 'my moving syndrome. In the last eight years that I've lived in the city (Manhattan), I think I've moved about seven times.' His Upper East Side apartment on Park Avenue was also invaded by an admiring press.

He talked, too, about his schooldays, telling one interviewer, 'My teachers all loathed me. I never did homework. I'm amazed to this day that they really expected me to go home and work on those sleazy projects that they had outlined.' His parents, too: 'They were called to school so often that my friends still recognise them on the street. Even now, they'd feel much better if I had lived up to their dream and been a pharmacist. There's tremendous pressure where I come from – a middle-class Jewish neighbourhood – to be an optometrist or a dentist or a lawyer, and that's what my friends have become.'

There was no mention of Mickey Rose, who had *not* become any of these things. Woody was already shaping the persona he had chosen for himself as the lone-star eccentric, the one who'd got away.

So, few wrung from him, as did Helen Dudar, the less exciting facts that he had 'managed to get through public school, his bar mitzvah and high school, but survived only three months of college before NYU dropped him, and had an even shorter spell at CCNY (New York's City College).' To Dudar he also went so far as to discuss, briefly, the failure of his marriage to Harlene. 'I'm glad I was married,' he told her. 'In that time, I put my wife through college. It really blossomed her. And I count it as an extremely valuable experience for me. It introduced me to a million things I probably wouldn't have known about.'

If Woody was thinking of the reaction he was getting to those sour reflections of his on Harlene's 'blossoming' marriage, it's doubtful if his divorced wife would have agreed that it had been such a 'valuable experience'. The marriage, whichever way Harlene looked at it, had been a failure. Woody's career on the other hand was taking off like the rockets pointing skywards at Cape Kennedy.

Most significantly today, Woody's entry in *American Who's Who* ignores completely his marriage to Harlene. The years she shared, when they had little more than their joint love of jazz and recorders, are not even mentioned.

Alright already

At this point, however, something of Harlene's influence had begun to mature in him. Seeds of cultural appreciation and interest which had taken root seem to have flowered in his awakening consciousness. Books such as he had scornfully rejected at Midwood now fascinated him. According to his father, Woody rarely went out of his apartment without diving into a bookshop and coming out with an armful of heavy volumes. As Marty Konigsberg told an interviewer: 'Woody's filling his head with everything that's ever been written.' He added: 'God knows when he finds time for it all!'

Time, however, was expandable. Reportedly, Woody was finding it unnecessary to sleep more than six or seven hours a night, and would wake and read voraciously through the pile of books by his bed. 'Dr. Johnson and James Boswell are my heroes right now,' he told William K. Zissner.

At the same time he was said to be running literary marathons through such heavyweight thickets as Kafka and Schopenhauer, Kierkegaard and Sigmund Freud. To quench this hot stream of culture, he'd douse himself with the blood-and-guts of Ernest Hemingway. Reading how others wrote had apparently become an obsession; the world of ideas, written and spoken, was opening a golden door to his development.

Helen Dudar first noticed it, shrewdly dubbing him 'an erudite mouse'. It was a neat description of what he had almost perfected as a transformation from the *nebbish* of early days: in private, a solemn, even owlish debater, capable – with disarmingly accurate recall of everything read, seen and heard – of cutting far better-versed viewpoints down to well below their accustomed stature. His greatest use of this expanding vision, needless to say, was in his work.

To Joanne Stang of the *New York Times* Woody confided that he had no idea why people rated him an intellectual comic. 'I can't tell you what I am,' he said. 'But I can tell you what I'm *not*. I'm not "fey" and I'm not "Chaplinesque". And above all I'm not "cerebral". Why does a pair of glasses automatically make you "cerebral"? Sex and death are two fairly elementary subjects, and they are my two biggest themes – because they interest me the most. My reactions to everyday situations seem normal to me, but completely hilarious to everyone else. And most of the time I can't figure out why.'

But, by writing them down, by expressing what he felt and thought on paper, he could at least create his vision of the world without interference. Seemingly alone now, except for a succession of lady friends who rarely lasted long or achieved any degree of intimacy with him, he turned his insatiable appetite for work towards plays, films, skits and articles. At the *New Yorker* magazine to which he submitted a succession of his better pieces, he was recognised and published in 1965.

Some of Woody's later articles were rejected by the magazine, but he was too bright a gem to discard lightly. The first piece they accepted was a gloriously funny sketch of two chess players corresponding with each other during a game played by mail. Roger Angell, the senior editor of the magazine who handled Woody's copy then (and still does, seventeen years later) saw its brilliance and spoke up for it in the weekly conference. 'There was no doubt in anybody's mind here,' he says, 'but that we'd discovered a very funny writer, of which there simply are not enough these days.'

Angell is a thick-set man with a solid grey moustache which adds strength to an already distinguished face. Spectacles set off his balding, rounded head. In the world of

American magazine publishing he is a highly respected figure. Woody and he got along famously.

'He's extremely hard-working,' Angell says. 'I would quite believe he has established a habit of writing for two or three hours every day whatever else he is doing. That is something we have never discussed, but I would imagine it might well be true of him.'

At first, though, there was a difficulty about Woody's style. It too closely resembled one of his idols of literary humour, S. J. Perelman. 'Obviously he was greatly influenced by him,' Angell says. 'Woody, I know, admired Perelman extravagantly. And Sid Perelman's language is recognisable in almost everything he wrote for us in the early years. I had to point that out to him.'

The picture of Woody, highly paid writer of comedy material for many of the nations's top stars, now an actor and scriptwriter for a smash-hit film and a well paid performer in his own right, having to be taught fresh techniques of writing is fascinating. Angell is not a man to have spared his feelings, or been impressed by his public stature. The *New Yorker* in its time has published many of America's greatest writers and tends to see itself as rather superior to any of them. At least mere money has never been the reward for which their contributors could be said to have come in search.

'I suppose we probably paid him a thousand dollars for that first piece (*The Gossage-Vardebedian Papers*) and it won't have changed much over the years,' Angell says with lordly detachment. 'We don't pay a great deal. Writers as a whole like to write for us, and I'm sure Woody does it for that reason and no other. So far as we are concerned, that is.'

But the Perelman similarity was an embarrassment. 'I told him, "Look, we already have one Perelman!" And he took it rather well. Just the same, it's a very hard thing for any writer to change his style. It took Woody quite a long while to get Sid's mannerisms out of his system.'

When he did, as Angell admiringly acknowledges, Woody found a technique very much his own. 'Five years later,' Angell says, 'we had a piece from him – it was called

111

A Look at Organised Crime – which was completely different from anything Perelman could have written. And very, very funny.'

Woody had found a unique personal formula to the complete satisfaction of Roger Angell and his colleagues. As, over the years, he has for the magazine's devoted readers. Yet for himself it seems that no peak is ever a summit.

Those articles, now collected and published as books, show that he was letting his wryest thoughts flow onto paper. 'His manuscripts are always neatly typed when they reach me,' says Angell, 'though whether he does them or some secretary of his agent, Rollins and Joffe, I couldn't say.' In fact, most of his work is said to pass through Norma-Lee's efficient hands. The wall above her desk, decorated with five blown-up 'mug-shots' of Woody, shows how closely they work together.

It is Norma-Lee, Woody's faithful amanuensis, who checks and corrects the slightest slip and error in his *New Yorker* stories before sending them on. Woody has admitted that his own spelling and grammar are often appalling. Yet even she cannot get it right every time, and Roger Angell tells a revealing story.

New Yorker editorial policy is largely arrived at by concensus and chance. 'People often imagine we set a theme for each issue,' Angell explains. 'Not at all. Our writers make the theme for us. We just select and follow.'

Thus the need for each contributor to establish a strong, recognisable style and viewpoint – in Woody's case, his mockery of fundamentals – is of considerable importance both to the writer and the magazine. Meetings at which each separate issue is planned, concentrate on finding a key-note among the work submitted from which to build a structure for the whole edition.

On this occasion the conference was in favour of using a masterly piece by Woody – who attends most of the meetings – so as to offset the main theme. The story, titled *The Diet*, satirises the importance of self-sacrifice in restricting an appetite for rich foods. Its Kafkaesque description of a father condemning his éclair-addicted son to death for giv-

112

ing in to his appetite is so heavily surrealistic that almost any behaviour by the main characters would be acceptable.

'But the last line seemed misplaced to me,' Angell remembers. 'I mentioned it to Woody and he took it away at once. It's always his way. He'll adapt any piece without hesitation, provided he does it himself. Nobody else must tinker with it. He'll do whatever we ask him to, if we think it necessary. And sometimes, as a result of little changes, I've read stuff of Woody's that has made me helpless with laughter.'

To look into Roger Angell's quietly serious eyes behind their spectacles, to examine the lines of sober maturity in his face, is to recognise that whatever makes him laugh helplessly must indeed have extraordinary powers. As an editor, he is well-known to be painstakingly precise and demanding, characteristics which led to the denouement of his tale about Woody:

'Well, I had to turn it back to him a second time,' he says, 'because it still wasn't quite right. When I told Woody this he promised to send me three or four endings to choose from. And that's what he did.

'The one I immediately liked read: "The two agreed and resolved to spend more time with otters." I thought this extremely funny. Exactly what the piece needed.'

Angell leans back in his chair, savouring the recollection. The light streaming through the window of his small office near New York's Museum of Modern Art strikes his rotund head, giving it the look of a Roman anger about to examine the entrails of geese.

'When I phoned Woody to say so, though,' he says with a light chuckle, 'he said "But that's not the line I wrote!" Apparently he had written out the endings for me in long-hand and handed them to somebody to type who couldn't read his writing. "It must be a typographical error," he said over the telephone. "I wrote *others* not *otters!*" '

Would he change it to *otters*, to please his august editor? He would not. 'I tried to make him accept *otters*, which seemed so much funnier to me,' Angell admits, 'but he wouldn't do it. It went in as *others*.' As anyone who possesses a copy of

113

old *New Yorker* files, or of Woody's book *Side Effects* may check for themselves on page 68. *Others* it firmly is.

This sort of controlling influence by experienced editors seems to have been exactly what Woody needed. Perhaps it was a stone he trusted to rub off exesses and repair insufficiences in his prose. Angell and his colleagues operated a benign but impartially severe discipline which no persuasions, such as the eminence of a contributor or the popularity of his work elsewhere, could affect in the slightest.

'Of course we have had to turn down some of his material,' Angell says of Woody's work. 'If the other editors who read it think it isn't funny I have to tell him so. He's very flexible, and indeed modest about what he writes. When you consider how extensive his career and achievements have been it is an admirable thing that he is.'

Today, Woody is finding less and less time to write for the magazine, which Roger Angell and his confederates of the editorial oligarchy deeply regret. 'He has let us have rather less pieces in recent years,' he says unhappily. 'I only wish he could find time to contribute more. Woody Allen is one of our funniest writers.'

He is also, of course, one of the world's funniest entertainers. Early in 1964, a year before the magazine accepted his first story for publication, *New York Daily News* reporter May Okon described him as 'the hottest comic on the showbusiness scene today.' Woody was then struggling with his first play in draft form. Sketches of ideas were floating in his head, forming patterns for future films, plays and pieces. The more bizarre the notion, the more it tickled his fancy.

And the world was opening up for him. Work on *Pussycat* had been unhappy and frustrating, but Feldman's extravagant habit of sending his writers and film crews in all directions in search of locations had provided a taste of lands and cities far beyond Brooklyn, Manhattan or even Los Angeles and the American cities he had performed in.

With Charles Joffe as administrative chaperone, Woody was given glimpses of European capitals, visiting London,

Rome and Paris. Not that he actually saw much of them, or identified with their life-styles. His hotel room isolations were already pronounced. The story that he ordered and ate the same meal for dinner every night of his six-week stay in Paris – lightly-cooked sole – testifies to an extraordinary aversion to sampling any unknown dish.

There was nevertheless time to enjoy recreation now and again. The financial compensations for having subjected himself to Feldman's Hollywood switchback ride were becoming refreshingly evident. Following his divorce, settlement with Harlene presumably made it all the more necessary for him to seek a fair return for his work. Yet at the same time he was able to repay something of the debt he must have felt he still owed his parents, by sending them to tour five countries at his expense. It no doubt gave them almost as much pleasure as surprise: that his employment, in such a risky and ephemeral world as showbusiness, should have merited such rewards.

For relaxation, there was always jazz. His technique as a clarinetist (who could also, on occasion, double on alto saxophone) was well exercised if not great. While never destined to reach the top flight of virtuoso instumentalists, Woody – in the opinion of those who knew – wasn't at all bad. In December '63, he reportedly appeared with the Count Basie orchestra at Carnegie Hall, blowing a few, modest riffs with noticeable enjoyment. The use of music as therapy ancillary to his weekly psycho-analytic treatments was already pronounced.

Curiosity also seems to have marked his activities. In his apartment on Park Avenue at 74th Street, he once proudly showed a journalist the huge telescope with tripod and reflector through which, as he explained, it would be possible to study the stars, 'if only I could see anything from here except a brick wall.'

But he was living alone, and there were signs of restlessness which close friends noticed.

Standing in for Johnny Carson on the popular *Tonight* television show can hardly have been a complete substitute for the love and companionship which had gone out of his

life with Harlene. Other women seem to have been trans-
ient partners at best, capable of soothing only briefly the
yearning he no doubt felt – now more strongly than ever –
for a mate who would not only respond to his physical but
also his mental needs and pursuits. Even the fame which
had culminated in a *Life Magazine* profile in August 1964
offered an irksome reminder that he was more satisfied
publicly than privately. It was inevitable that he would
meet a woman who could alter this situation; and he did so
with Louise Lasser, an actress. To everyone who really
knew him, it was an understandable match.

How he found time to woo her was a mystery. Certainly conventional morality had never impeded Woody's
lifestyle. At school, as he told Sidney Fields, 'I once turned
in a composition on *How I Spent My Summer Vacation* by
vividly describing a lush blonde I'd admired from a distance. The conclusion read: "This girl had a child by a
future marriage".' On that occasion, says Fields, 'the
school sent for Woody's mother'. But it failed to change his
views, which remain today uninhibited to say the least.

Indeed, he was developing tastes which remarkably
foreshadow his later life. One of the ladies he most admired
in the mid-60's was his actress companion of the '80s, Mia
Farrow. His openly flouted interest in such leading film
stars as Brigitte Bardot and Julie Christie was later
confirmed by an unusual taste for similar pampered beings.
Most directors, and particularly those with Woody's high
standards of intelligence and wit, avoid actresses. He
seems to court them.

Louise was in rather a different category. The daughter of
a leading tax accountant she had enjoyed a good education,
and an anything but needy upbringing. Woody and she
were chiefly attracted to one another, friends believe,
because of their individual eccentricities. Louise is often
described by those who enjoy her companionship as
'spaced out'. In her case, the expression is intended to
mean neurotic and 'wacky'. Liable on occasion to say and
do wild things.

Woody had kept his relationship with her remarkably

secret, a technique he developed then and has perfected since. Few outside his personal coterie of close friends knew even that he was friendly with her. He talked incessantly to inquisitive reporters about the women he ogled and desired, never about those who actually shared his pillow. Louise was the first of a long line of very private encounters with attractive women, none of whom has ever admitted to any great feeling of loss when their relationship, as inevitably has occurred, has been eclipsed by a successor.

Louise, however, was in the same line of work, which made a major difference. Also, she appears never to have bored or irritated Woody. Their mutual empathy seems to have sprung largely from her delight in his originality and irreverence; his for her understanding of what he was saying in all that he wrote and performed. The most natural outcome of their affaire, was a desire to stay together permanently: though how they managed to fit marriage into their busy schedules (which they did on 2 February 1966, with Woody rushing on after the ceremony to perform at a Manhattan hotel) is far from easy to imagine. Louise's family undoubtedly had to be considered; and certainly Woody's parents.

Louise had one immediate and remarkable effect on Woody. The recluse who had always shunned social life suddenly announced that he and his bride were hosting a Christmas party at their New York home. Not only Woody's select circle of friends, but hundreds of celebrity acquaintances were invited. If Woody and Louise had not disappeared to spend most of the evening in a hamburger bar, his reputation as a social hermit would have been lost. More understandably, another consequence of the marriage was Louise's role in one of the most demonstrative of Woody's films, What's Up Tiger Lily? In it, he made the first and truest statement of his attitude to the real world he mocked. The film spoofed everything in sight, including itself (an Oriental crime drama, over-dubbed with Woodyana dialogue and comic inter-cutting). It plainly showed its creator to be a complete outsider.

Tiger Lily, indeed, scoffed at the entire conventional world. It gave Woody's prismatic vision full rein. Using a number of recognisably Jewish verbal tricks, it threw up a Goon-like satire on a background of wholly farcical melodrama. Its chief creator was able to reveal for the first time his total lack of commitment to society's most cherished values.

The message, for all *Tiger Lily's* spoof of blood, torture and death, was hope. A generation born under the nuclear mushroom raised their hearts to it. They accepted this new prophet as one of their own.

Louise, Mickey Rose and another friend, Len Maxwell, enjoyed this romp with Woody, while he appears to have used them as sounding boards. The script was a series of impromptu inventions, often during the actual shooting in Teacher's Sound Studio on Broadway. Nobody was making a fortune from the movie, which lessened the pressure to take the thing seriously. Anyway, it was never intended as more than one of Filmland's private jokes: a whim of Hollywood producer Hank Saperstein.

How it began was that Saperstein, for his company American International, had bought a film made in Japan. A laughable, but absolutely straight, emulation of a James Bond 007 epic. Woody was invited, soon after he and Louise had begun their honeymoon-less marriage, to remove the Japanese soundtrack entirely from the film and substitute comic English. In doing so, he cut in entirely new scenes, using his own script and music. He himself made four telling appearances, once in silhouette making love to Louise in a projection booth.

The final film, which Maurice Yacowar, professor of English and Film at a Canadian university, has praised as 'the essential Woody Allen work', set Woody's life and attitudes on the screen for all to see.

Woody, said Yacowar, 'stands apart from the game of life (in the film) and jokes about the players.' Two of the star players in Woody's own game of life were Louise and himself. But others – those few intimates permitted entry into his personal circle – were already becoming part of his creative team.

Also, in the fresh dawn of his new marriage, Woody was showing signs of conscience if not remorse over the bad jokes he had been making in his act: those suggesting that his marriage to Harlene had been little more than tiresome tyranny. To Earl Wilson, the famed New York columnist who had first printed his schoolboy gags, he now made a remarkable admission. The gags about his marriage, he said, 'seem suddenly dated'.

What prompted this burst of self-analysis has never been revealed, but Harlene's feelings about those crude and cruel jokes have. The following spring of 1967 she sued both Woody and NBC for one million dollars in defamation damages. Woody's entire earnings up to that time had come to little more.

For *Tiger Lily* he had received only $75,000. The unpalatable *Pussycat* earned him less than half that sum. His nightclub earnings were now in the region of $1,000 a week, and occasional publications brought in enough to cover the rent of the two-level brownstone on 79th Street into which he and Louise had moved. When the American *Current Biography* of 1966 described him as 'perhaps the most prosperous of today's comedians' they were no doubt exaggerating.

But potentially he *was* rich. The enormous cascade of money flowing into box offices wherever Feldman's *Pussycat* was billed had established scriptwriter Woody Allen as an economic miracle worker. In Hollywood, he was credited with a gilt-edged reputation. It would last as long as his ability to turn in profitable screenplays. And remarkable evidence of this right to open-credit is that *since then not one of the fourteen pictures Woody Allen has been associated with has ever lost money.* Some, as Jack Rollins admits, have yet to make sizeable profits. But all have satisfied their backers.

So Charles Feldman faced a very differently placed Charles Joffe when he went back to Woody's managers to seek a further contract for his services. *Pussycat* had opened in New York in June 1965, a year previously. Woody's dream of becoming a director 'some day' – which he'd voiced with-

119

out any real hope of attainment to the *Midwood Argus* – was actually in sight.

'I would like to do films, write them, direct them, appear in them,' he now told a reporter confidently. 'I think I could direct films in my sleep. It's an inborn thing.'

Feldman was not prepared to go so far. But he did offer Woody a small part in *Casino Royale* on the strength of the torrent of success they had jointly, if not always harmoniously, accomplished. Sadly, it was to be another experience for Woody of a picture made for the lowest level of mass appreciation at its absolute worst. Not even the acting of David Niven could extricate *Casino Royale* from a miasma of deathly improbabilities and contrived fantasies. The film's humour – even Woody's noticeable, though uncredited, attempts – was submerged in trivia.

But Feldman, for all his extinction of Woody's injections of subtlety and wit, was still a goose capable of laying twenty-four-carat eggs. In May 1966 he took Woody's script of an unproduced play he had written, entitled *Take the Money and Run*, and tried to set up a deal with United Artists to make a film of it. It might have worked. But this time Charles Joffe was the obstacle. He stood firm, demanding director and main actor roles for Woody, as well as his script.

After more than a year of nail-biting haggles, Hollywood bowed. A studio called Palomar Pictures agreed to put up $1.6 million, with Joffe as the film's producer and Woody wearing his three-role hat. It showed enormous, if rash, courage by the backers since both Woody and Joffe were unknowns in their new fields. But *Pussycat* magic had spread over everyone connected, and the deal was done. Woody walked onto his first set as director admitting later, 'I didn't know the first thing.'

How news of this leap to glory reached Flatbush is still remembered by old neighbours and friends of the Konigsbergs. Woody's mother was still working. She'd kept the job she'd turned her hand to when things were tight, when Marty was driving a cab. Commuting to Manhattan daily by subway, Nettie was a valued book-keeper for a florist. Marty, back in his old job once more as an engraver of jewellery, sometimes travelled with her on his way to Eldridge Street.

In the evenings, they would invite friends in to watch 'our son Alan' doing his comic routines. Woody was appearing on major television shows which were now consistently inviting him to be their guest.

People who knew the Konigsbergs well at that time are anxious not to trade on their connection with what Woody has since become. But one of the friends, a man who shared those parentally proud evenings, saw something germinating then which has not changed: Woody's mother and father's distaste for some of his jokes.

'It wasn't that they didn't like them. They didn't understand them, I don't think,' he says. 'We lived two houses away on Avenue K. Woody's pretty sister Letty, who married a psychologist (now head teacher of an elementary public school in Brooklyn) about that time, had been to our house many times. She used to babysit for us. So we got to know the family and heard a lot about Woody.

'Mrs Konigsberg always kind of scared me, because, you know what? When Woody says (as he does in public and on film) that she looks like Groucho Marx, she does! But she always was very nice to me.

'I was a kid about the same age as Woody, maybe a bit younger. I remember his first appearance on the Jack Paar show. I think the whole neighbourhood in Flatbush must have been watching that night. Mrs Konigsberg had let it be known Woody was on.

'We were invited along to see it at their house, which was well situated on the corner with a piece of lawn all round it. Quite a nice house, but nothing fancy you understand. Anyway, they had a television set and we sat around and watched Woody do his act, which was really very funny. I was in stitches.

'Then I looked over at Mrs Konigsberg and it seemed to me she didn't know whether to be pleased or not. She wasn't laughing, and I remember wondering why. Later, I heard that Woody had upset Jack Paar that night, because a couple of his jokes were too off-colour for the sponsor, or the network. I guess it was that which had turned Mrs Konigsberg off them.

'We knew when he didn't appear with the rest of the guests. There was always a line-up on Paar's dais after the show was over. So something had misfired. It turned out, I believe, that Woody had really upset Paar because he'd refused to let him censor his stuff in advance.

'We heard from Mrs Konigsberg that this wasn't the first time, either. Once, so she told us, Woody had walked off a show – this must have been around 1959 or 60 – because they'd bleeped out the word "WC".'

To Marty and Nettie it may have seemed unnecessary for any son of theirs to make jokes in public which a nice well-brought up Jewish boy wouldn't make in his own home. There has always been a strong hint of Woody's sharpest mockeries being reserved for established Jewish attitudes and customs. To the orthodox and narrow-minded, as to the highly cultured defenders of Jewish tradition, such satirising of his birthright is unseemly.

Art d'Lugoff runs the Village Vanguard today, where once Woody performed for Feldman. He and old-timers like Joe Franklin, one of the kindest, most helpful of New York's showmen (his radio show *Down Memory Lane* does enormous good for the morale of artists who are forgotten by today's audiences) have professional regard for Woody's talent. They see him as a genius of comedy. But d'Lugoff, certainly, and several others in varying degree (depending on their orthodoxy) shy away from some of his cracks at their customs.

'Deep down he doesn't understand Judaism or Jewishness,' d'Lugoff says. 'It upsets me, always has. He can't accept his parents' middle-classness, he equates it with Jewishness in a very anti-semitic way.

'He pokes fun at the grossness of the middle-class, as if that was essentially a Jewish characteristic. Actually, it's the same in all races. They all climb on the same ladder.

'Woody won't see that. He didn't have the background that I did, you see. I had a college education and come from a very orthodox family, while he's probably the first of his family to be educated properly. And he didn't learn much at school from what I've heard.

'He didn't learn to speak Yiddish, or Jewish, of that I'm almost certain. I come from the same place, so I know. Flatbush was my home too. But he's thrown all that away.'

Art d'Lugoff, a tall, darkly sober man in late middle-age, lets the severity in his eyes relax as personal memories of Woody and the days they worked together return to his mind.

'Yes, he was touched by all those things I was,' he says. 'And I just hope in time he gets closer to his roots, to Jewish history. Why does he hate it so? I suppose because his interests are and always were so different from those around him. He was the *nebbish* when young. I mean, is it an accident that in recent years he has gone for non-Jewish girls – and not particularly brainy ones? Just pretty to look at.'

He doesn't wait for an answer because, to d'Lugoff the question answers itself. No 'good' Jewish boy mixes – especially not in marriage – with *shiksas* (Hebrew for 'blemish'), as Christian women and Jewish women who do not keep a *kosher* home are called by the orthodox.

'I've got a son, a twenty-two-year-old redhead, who imitates Woody,' he says. 'He's very funny. Very caustic and wry, I could almost believe it was Woody at that age. But he didn't like his latest picture, *Stardust Memories*, one bit. I did. To me it has a lot more, I don't know. . .'

He pauses. Thinks for a while. Then continues thoughtfully: 'I think Woody shows in that movie that he is finding his way back, maybe. He makes a lot of keen observations in it which could add up to that.'

Which, if true, would please Art d'Lugoff and no doubt many other good Jewish people including Woody's parents a whole lot. Marty and Nettie keep quiet about their feelings. When Woody portrays families like his own on screen as vulgar and eccentric, puts false noses and Groucho moustaches and spectacles on parents, they suffer it in silence.

But those who know the Konigsbergs are not fooled.

As soon as he could afford it, Woody moved his parents to Manhattan's Upper East Side. A good neighbourhood, one might imagine he chose it to provide them with some of the better things of life which had been lacking in his childhood. In fact, he probably wanted to sever any remaining cords binding him to a part of the world he dislikes almost as much as he dislikes the open air: Brooklyn's Flatbush.

To make them comfortably better off was certainly his wish. In the same way he used one of his comically-named companies, Hackenbush Productions (after Groucho Marx's famed character) to shield their identity when he bought them an apartment on South Ocean Drive, Hallandale, one of Florida's choice districts. His father, now past eighty, and his mother spend half the year down there in the sunshine. By the time they come back to New York, in late spring, the weather is warm and their family delighted to see them.

Woody's sister and her husband lead busy lives. Apart from looking after her husband, Sidney, during the term times of his Brooklyn School, Letty Aronson has worked in television, helping to create some of the shows put on by Woody's long-time friend Jean Doumanian. Jean's production of the once-popular *Saturday Night Live* ended abruptly last spring (1981), but Woody's many contracts should guarantee his sister more and better projects.

So the Konigsbergs, an active if elderly couple, are able to see their successful children for only a small part of New York's long hot summer. Like all elderly mothers, Nettie no doubt wishes it was more often. There is nothing strange about that, or about Nettie and her husband. The one surprising thing is that Marty still keeps his hand in at his old job, working with an old friend called Jack Roth. Like Woody, he finds a vital therapy in keeping busy.

Jack Roth is related to the Konigsbergs by marriage, a distant alliance of cousins. His jewellery business is a small narrow shop, Richards Jewels, at 789 Lexington Avenue in the centre of New York. Thirty years or so ago he first met

Marty at the wedding of those relatives. He learned then that they were both in the same business.

'Before I knew him he'd been a waiter down there in the Bowery,' Roth says, 'but I think, then, he was already getting back into jewellery. Years later, when he found he had spare time on his hands, he came in here and started giving me a little help.' Martin Koningsberg doesn't do too much, says Roth, but 'he keeps busy and is a very active man. You can't keep up with him sometimes.'

Woody's picture used to hang on Jack Roth's shop wall. He took it down when customers asked too many questions. 'I don't get to talk to Woody all that much,' he explains. 'He's a very shy guy, and he won't come in here even when his father's working with me. My cousin tells me that he's like that everywhere. Even when the family has little gatherings, or when his mother has a few people up to her apartment, he'll just say hallo, then disappear into a bedroom and watch television. Or maybe he'll spend a few minutes with them and then leave. He doesn't care to be with even his own family for too long, I guess.'

Marty, on the other hand, is sociable. He enjoys chatting to Jack and others who share his interest. He is deeply proud of his son. 'His birthday is Christmas Day,' Jack Roth says, 'and he was eighty in 1979, so he must have been around thirty-five when Woody was born. I tell you he hasn't done any jewellery engraving for years, though Woody always says that's what his father does.'

Woody, Jack says, ribs his parents all the time. So how does this go down with them? 'They don't seem to mind, but I'll tell you this: they don't always see the funny side.' As Roth says, Woody is very good to his mother and father. They can afford to forgive him a lot.

Marty, says Roth, goes to see all his son's films. 'Not always on first nights. He just goes in when he feels like it, and pays for a ticket like anybody else. A lot of it, he likes. He gets a good laugh out of it.'

But not all? 'Well no,' Jack admits. 'Sometimes he'll come back and tell me, "You know, Jack, I don't understand that son of mine. I don't understand that crap he's writing!"'

Jack Roth has his own views of how Nettie sees Woody, based on observations over the years. 'But she doesn't say a word against him, naturally,' he says. 'I'd say she is real proud of Woody – though I'm not saying she wouldn't have been happier if he'd made good in some other career.' He laughs. 'You know, *my son, the doctor*! They say that's why there are too many doctors in New York, don't they? Because of all the Jewish mothers!'

One thing Jack's knowledge of the Konigsbergs makes him sure about: Woody's talent is not noticeably inherited. 'I can't think of anyone remotely connected with him who has the least touch of Woody's comic genius,' he says. 'Or anyone who made it so good. I mean, he's worth millions . . .' Jack looks ruefully round his small-shop where he and Woody's father spend long hours peering through magnifying glasses at pieces of jewellery worth less than Woody earns in a few minutes '. . . while I'm breaking my back to make a living!'

In one of the few straight-faced interviews he has given, Woody is quoted by Edwin Miller of *Seventeen* magazine as endorsing much of what Jack Roth has said. The article, which appeared in May 1966 just three months after Woody's second marriage, has Woody talking of his parents. They had disapproved of his divorce from Harlene and were still recovering from his marriage to an actress about whom they knew next-to-nothing, except that she had understudied Barbra Streisand in *I Can Get It For You Wholesale*. Woody, apparently speaking with conviction if not total accuracy, told Miller:

'My parents enjoy my success. They enjoy seeing my name in columns and me appearing on television and making movies like *Casino Royale* . . . But all this makes them somewhat uneasy. They would be much happier if I quit it all today and went to college and studied to be a pharmacist and went to work and made a hundred and twenty-five dollars a week for the rest of my life. With a pension.

'They never have been able to shake the feeling of imminent catastrophe. That's the way they grew up.'

Revealingly, Woody admitted to a similar fantasy himself. 'I always have a fear of being shot,' he explained. 'By a girl, a psychotic fan who imagines some connection between us.' In his recent film *Stardust Memories* he uses a similarly dramatic sequence.

John Lennon's death, which occurred *after* this sequence was filmed, made it chillingly prophetic.

From that he makes a living?

Marriage to Louise, meanwhile, was providing them both with the illusion of living on air and dreams. She confessed 'We're like two kids in a castle,' which was not far from the truth. Having escaped from the constraints of having to perform his 'husband bit' for Harlene, Woody plunged into Bohemian casualness. Valuable paintings, acquired in London and elsewhere (largely from poker winnings, though he later gave up the game completely) leaned haphazardly against walls. Neither Woody nor Louise possessed any strongly defined domestic skills. Armed with a hammer, Woody was considered by everyone who knew him to be potentially lethal.

In one favourite room of their spacious high-ceilinged old apartment, the faded grandeur was relieved only by an American billiard table. An original Kokoschka still had to be hung. The incongruity of such works of fine art alongside fruit machines, a jukebox, an electric organ and cases of Woody's soda-pop, totally escaped the newlyweds.

It was a period of creative expansion such as he had never before been able to afford. Woody wrote, among the dissarray of expensive junk, with absolute detachment. Semi-seriously, he tried his hand at oil painting while rarely moving out of range of his one abstraction: scenes of autumn with surrealistic overtones. One, entitled *Autumn Camel* (containing a television screen) was inexplicably linked to the desert in winter.

But rewards for his real work were growing quite fabulously, the money rolling in. In that year, 1966, Woody's personal till rang up a quarter of a million dollars from his

128

work on the films *Casino Royale* and *Tiger Lily*, his play-writing, his *New Yorker* publications, television appearances and performances. Like Jack Roth and his father, Woody was incapable of sitting still.

By early 1967, he was writing the screenplay for his first film as director *Take the Money and Run*, while at the same time nursing his Broadway success *Don't Drink the Water* to a highly successful eighteen-month run and a popular film. Max Gordon, to his dismay, had decided the play had no merit after persuading Woody to write it. Producer David Merrick took it two days after Woody handed it to him, changed the title (originally Woody had called it *Yankee, Come Home*), insisted on changes in script and cast (in all there were twelve changes, a historical first) before bringing it to Broadway. Despite the fact that they fought constantly, Merrick finally achieved all Woody could have hoped for.

All in all, 1967 was another hectic year. The play had opened at the Morosco Theatre in mid-November 1966 starring Lou Jacobi and Kay Medford. Leading critic Richard Watts Junior panned it, but others were kinder. Two weeks later Woody, who had had nothing to do with the play other than write it (and was actually playing pool with Mickey Rose on opening night), flew to Las Vegas to appear at Caesar's Palace for a two-week date.

The act was the same. 'I draw from twelve to fifteen different routines and usually go on for thirty-five minutes,' Woody told Miller. 'I draw my material from things that happen to me, like my parents, my school, marriage. Some of it is true, some of it isn't. I don't care which as long as it gets a laugh.'

The only drawback, as Woody was discovering ('I can make awful mistakes . . . stories about being divorced in front of a college crowd') lay in what other people – notably Harlene – felt. And how much she cared when he tossed poisoned barbs at his sometimes true, sometimes imagined marriage. Her lawsuit followed requests through her lawyers for Woody to tone down or cut out altogether these damaging digs. Yet, and in spite of what he had told *New*

York Post columnist Wilson, Woody persisted.

On both the Jack Carson and Perry Como shows – networked across the United States – Woody again used wisecracks stemming ostensibly from his first marriage.

In these sideswipes Woody was exercising his artistic right to satirise the state of marriage. His target was the whole of conventional society, not one unhappy woman. But the effect was to bring such distress to Harlene that she took him to court, not once but twice.

On the second occasion the suit had doubled its price ticket to two million dollars. Jeremiah Gutman, Harlene's lawyer in New York, maintains that Harlene as a result of the divorce arrangements, has been left in no great shape financially. 'The fact is she is poor. A struggling fine artist, painting in oils.' She has loyally refused, nevertheless, to sell her story of life with Woody to the press. Those who know the first Mrs Allen believe she may still nurse what the French call a *'tendresse'* for her ex-husband, although it is doubtful if she has been in more than passing contact with him for twenty years.

Fortunately, there were no children by either marriage. The carefree Elysium of sharing his existence with Louise may have increased Woody's creative output, but it did nothing to alter his diffidence about accepting a family as his own. (The big question around his circle of friends during 1981, when he was seen constantly in the company of the beautiful and twice-married American actress, Mia Farrow, was how Woody would cope with the seven children Mia has in her care, her own and those she has adopted.)

Equally doubtful is whether Woody agreed to pay Harlene a lump sum or regular alimony. The latter seems likelier, since Harlene has recently complained that inflation and the rising cost of living has made it hard for her to manage. Gutman will only reply to questions on this by reminding the questioner that he has never maintained that there *was* a lump sum paid to his client. It strongly suggests that Harlene today is on Woody's payroll, along with many others in his family and outside.

He was behaving, too, like a man who has to support more than one wife and family. Through Charles Joffe's efforts, his fee for a major television show appearance had risen to $10,000. At Caesar's Palace, according to *Time* magazine, he was paid $25,000 for a week. He had, as the paper said, also dashed off four comic essays for the *New Yorker* and turned out two bestselling comedy albums (records) of his monologues.

Woody also accepted completely out-of-character assignments during this period of intensive financial advancement. He signed a contract with the agents for Smirnoff Vodka, and was photographed in colour with busty filmstars Mamie Van Vooren and others for full-page advertisements in leading American magazines. Though his alcoholic intake has rarely exceeded Continental-style wine with meals, this did nothing to jar his ethos. In the same way he advertised a brand of sunglasses, while admitting to Earl Wilson that he never wore them himself 'because they change my perspective on the world'.

None of this dimmed or even blew steam on his image. The jester, now that his cult-following in the States had become not only firmly established but hungry for any scrap of Woodyana to appear, was assured an indestructible place. Everything he chose to do, however, bizarre, was alchemised. Rumour had it that he was earning a half a million dollars a year and this may have been an understatement. That year, 1967, he was rarely out of the public gaze.

Aside from the TV shows already mentioned, he wrapped up December as guest-host of NBC's *Kraft Music-Hall Hour* with Liza Minnelli and right-wing writer William F. Buckley Junior. As in an interview he later conducted with evangelist preacher Billy Graham, Woody showed he was masterful at handling heavy subjects. On Buckley he used wit, intelligence and extraordinary *chutzpa* (the markedly Jewish quality of insolent yet endearing gall) to avoid tangling with viewpoints and opinions he certainly did not share.

Politically, Woody likes to assert that he is wholly

uncommitted. If anything, he could be classed as a democratic left-wing republican, but nobody would bother – least of all his circle of close friends. To Woody, as to those around him, politics seem to be a sad and wearisome bore, not to be discussed soberly or be involved in.

In religion, he left no doubt in Dr Graham's mind that he is anything but agnostic. While keeping the popular preacher on his toes with some of the most direct and searching questions he has ever been faced with, Woody nevertheless managed to present an appearance of complete cordiality between the two. It was a splendid piece of visual stagecraft: the comic TV host at his best. Though whether Woody was joking when he afterwards confessed to Kay Gardella of the *New York Daily News* that 'frankly I'd love to be converted', is impossible to judge. To date, if that is truly his wish, he has shown little, if any, inclination towards it.

There was, however, more than a hint of humanitarianism in the stand he took against the Vietnam war. In October 1969 Woody was appearing on Broadway in his second play, *Play It Again Sam*. On the day when anti-war protesters called for support for their rally, Woody refused to go on. He has recently come out against the censorious attitudes of another preacher, the Reverend Jerry Falwell and his Moral Majority campaign, in much the same way as he took part in the anti-McCarthy film made in 1976 by Martin Ritt, *The Front*. In the event that opponents of extremism in any form had to stand up and be counted, all sixty-six inches of Woody would no doubt rise to the occasion.

Let it be said that there are aspects of existence which interest him more: sex for instance. Woody has perfected the image of the stunted, unlikely lover – the loser all men other than Adonises know themselves to be – succeeding in spite of himself. It is probably his greatest gift, one that immediately relates to the baffled multitudes of men who are incessantly told that 'this is the permissive age, the free-sex society', yet find it hard to get a girl they fancy to hold their hand in a cinema.

Woody calls on the whimsical, the magical and the gods of love to help even the runtiest, most inept males make it in the end. His Broadway play *Sam* was a delicious exposition of this theory, with Bogart always on hand to guide the inadequacies of the sexually repressed hero, played by Woody, towards a totally unexpected emotional climax with his best friend's wife, played by Diane Keaton.

The play had opened in February at New York's Broadhurst Theatre to the sort of notices which bring in audiences looking for nothing but a pleasant, amusing evening. Clive Barnes in the *New York Times* called it 'slender but hilarious', and John Chapman of the *Daily News* 'pleasantly daffy'. For Woody it was both a joy and an emotional experience. Diane Keaton had come into his life at exactly the moment when Cloud Nine with Louise Lasser was failing to support either of them.

Louise looks back on her years of marriage to Woody as sweet and pleasant. Their separation four months after *Sam* had opened was bloodless. The talk was that there would be no 'immediate divorce', and friends found no difficulty in accepting the break-up, as they had the marriage. 'Everybody loves them both,' one told columnist Earl Wilson, who broke the news of the end of the affair for this 'popular couple'.

Three months before, Wilson had been recording for posterity the not entirely unconnected story of how Woody had 'discovered' Miss Keaton.

Woody's way of casting is unique. For films he is known to prefer not to look at the actor or actress before him, examining instead their photograph and synopsis. Whether this is shyness or artistic 'distancing' he has never explained. In the theatre he is as happy with unknowns as with great stars, often favouring artistes he catches sight of in obscure plays and films rather than anyone with sufficient stature to make him feel inferior. Diane Keaton was appearing (with clothes *on*) in the almost all-nude show *Hair* when Woody noticed her.

'He'd gone to the show with Tony Roberts (leading Broadway actor starring in *Sam* with whom Woody had struck up a lasting friendship) and couldn't take his eyes off this girl,' a friend says. 'Diane was everything he had in mind for the leading role of his wife in the play.'

The one snag was her height. 'I'm five foot seven inches,' Diane said when he went backstage to ask if she'd play the part opposite him, 'how tall are you?'

Woody smiled weakly: 'Take your shoes off,' he told her, 'and we'll see.'

'Woody was wearing tennis shoes,' Diane remembers. 'I thought, surely I would be too tall for him. He looked like a little mole to me. But when we stood back to back there wasn't anything in it. We were roughly the same height.'

To Earl Wilson, who recorded all this, Diane confided that, in the play, Woody 'is the loser'. Weighing the warm glances she and Woody exchanged, the columnist ended his piece with a typical aside. 'Evidently,' he wrote, 'Woody is a loser only in this play.'

Diane and Woody were soon living together in an affaire which, long after it had burned itself out, was cementing a respectful and rewarding friendship. Diane's stumbling, self-critical ineptitude on screen in *Annie Hall* was the quality Woody first recognised in her as an answer to his awkwardness.

Gary Stevens who knows Diane well and finds her entirely likeable, is incapable of understanding their romance because 'they're so utterly different in every way'. He may be missing the essential point: that Diane Keaton sees the conventional world through the same prism as Woody Allen. They both find reality intimidating and take refuge in gentle mockery and self-searching (via repeated couch-sessions with their analysts).

'Don't ask me why she fell for him, I can't answer that, because I didn't know Adam and Eve,' says Stevens. 'But she's a sweet, fine actress and I can well understand what he saw in her.' Diane had glimpsed a side of Woody which touches many of those who get to know him intimately: his reluctance to see himself as important. His press agent for the last nineteen years, Richard O'Brien, will never forget his first example of it.

'It was during the release of *Pussycat*,' he says, 'when I'd set up an interview for him with Jack Gaver, drama critic of the *United Press*. I'd called Woody and told him we were to meet Jack at Manny Wolf's restaurant on Third Avenue at 48th Street.'

Long after the time for the appointment Woody had still not turned up. 'This was very surprising and worrying to me,' O'Brien says. 'He's always so punctual. So, finally, I went outside to look and see if I could spot him anywhere.'

And there was Woody, standing lamely in a telephone booth, trying to look as if he was searching for a number to dial.

'He'd come to the restaurant, asked for a table in my name, then gone outside again when they told him they didn't have a reservation in that name – I'd booked it in Woody's. It just never occurred to him that I'd use his name for anything as important as that! He was hanging about outside for maybe twenty minutes, thinking we were sure to turn up. I must say I find that very endearing.'

Those who find Woody endearing are on the way to earning his lasting support. Richard O'Brien's association with him dates back to Woody's earliest stand-up comic days, but it has deepened and enlarged. For the past fourteen years O'Brien has been writing jokes for Woody, some of which he uses in his films and routines.

'Only on the understanding that I never claim them as my own,' O'Brien says. 'Woody and I have a strictly business relationship, if a friendly one. He's a truly wonderful man – I've thought so from the beginning – and I'm proud to do what I can to help with his material.'

O'Brien's regular weekly production of some fifty or so gags and one-liners may not be all that Woody requires to fill any gaps left in his own steady output, but they obviously help. His loyal press agent friend also has a signed comic strip running in the *New York Daily News* – no doubt helped by Woody's influence. Five years ago Richard O'Brien gave up all other clients to work only for Woody. It was a decision he is never likely to regret.

In August 1969, with *Play It Again Sam* packing its

houses, and Diane Keaton taking up an increasingly large percentage of Woody's time and interest, his debut as a film director at last appeared on screen. *Take the Money and Run*, which he and his Midwood pal Mickey Rose had scripted so happily together, and which all of Charley Joffe's tenacity had finally given life to, was alive and kicking. It had been no easy birth.

Diane described Woody as 'acting like a scatterbrain on stage; but in fact an amazingly organised person, with an office, a secretary and a well-arranged schedule that he adheres to.' Others, like film editor (now director) Ralph Rosenblum, discovered he had so little patience with any part of his work that he would often sacrifice extremely funny material rather than attempt to 'patch or revise it in the cutting room'. His best babies, in other words, went the way of the bathwater.

Rosenblum was called in when *Take the Money* had been undergoing this whittling process for some eight months, with the result that much of the best material had been discarded. Fortunately it was not lost. And, as he describes in an unusually frank and detailed account of his association with Woody contained in his book *When the Shooting Stops, the Cutting Begins* (with Robert Karen, Viking, 1979), he was able to reintroduce and reshape much of the material.

As an established editor for twenty-five years, with major cutting experience, Rosenblum unquestionably saved Woody from disaster on this, his first directing assignment. It led to their making six pictures together, including *Annie Hall* which won Rosenblum a British Academy Award.

He left Woody before the making of *Stardust Memories* in 1980. But not, as people tend to think, because of any difference of opinion. 'Woody felt I was overqualified as an editor after all that time, and I had a great desire to leave the (cutting) room and move on.'

Woody is a director other technicians can or cannot relate to. Rosenblum says he enjoyed working with him. He sees him as a major film artist. Criticisms of their relationship, suggesting that Rosenblum lacked respect for Woody, and that he expects him to fail now that he is no longer editing his films, earn his bitter rejection.

'I don't want to say any more about it,' he exclaims. 'Our split was mutual. It's ridiculous to say that I don't admire his work. I'd hardly have stayed to make six pictures with him if I'd lacked all respect for the guy!'

Yet, at the time of their first association, Woody was an acutely worried man. He was closer to Diane that he had ever been to any woman he had worked and lived with. She had contributed to the punishing decisions which had resulted eventually in the battered, semi-lifeless rough-cut of *Take the Money* inherited by Ralph Rosenblum. And she saw his self-confidence ebbing fast.

'He sits at a typewriter for hours and hours a day,' she told Earl Wilson. 'He doesn't drink, eats very little meat, and his one indulgence is Orange Julius (a special form of soda-pop, based on fresh orange juice).'

Working with Diane on tour with *Play It Again Sam*, and then on Broadway, was some consolation for Woody. But the worry he felt about his film was making him hard to live with; let alone work with in the confines of a film cutting-room.

Rosenblum mentions one difficult collaboration Woody had which illustrates much of the problem. It was with composer Marvin Hamlisch, who wrote the music for *Take the Money*. His and Woody's temperaments were almost exact opposites. As a result, the tension between them created an atmosphere like an emotional powder-keg. Once, Rosenblum records, it exploded.

As he later heard the story from production manager Jack Grossberg, Hamlisch had written an original ballad to cover the main titles of the picture. The brilliant young composer was 'justifiably pleased' with it, says Rosenblum, which probably means that he was over the moon: Hamlisch is not a phlegmatic man.

Woody's reaction, when he heard the music, was utterly quenching on the other hand. He shrugged. As the last notes of Hamlisch's creation died away in the small theatre, director Woody Allen turned to ask, with obvious distaste:

'What was *that*?'

Rosenblum's account concludes with a scene which will be recognisable to many who still find it difficult to work with Woody today. 'When Allen left the room,' he says, 'Marvin lay down on the floor and wept.'

The problem of finding those who can stomach such treatment, yet produce original, creative work is common to many directors who are also, like Woody, shy individualists. While it has never been his intention to intimidate, few understand his extraordinarily severe method of selection. Or how deeply critical he can be of his own as well as other people's efforts.

'Woody is a serious writer,' Rosenblum explains. 'He's always saying he wants to "sit at the grown-ups" table! He wants to make serious films. He'll probably do it, too.'

Woody, as Ralph Rosenblum knows, is increasingly attacked for not sticking to the comedy formula of *Annie Hall, Manhattan* and (an attempt which many regard as a failure) *Stardust Memories.* This ex-editor's view is that it will not deter him from a more serious aim.

'If some people think he's not funny, that doesn't bother him at all,' he says. 'Nor do the people who tell him he should stick to comedy. He's a man who doesn't care what others think. He just goes on to the next subject as soon as he's finished with the last. In my experience of him he's always been like that. An eager learner who has become a major film director.'

The trouble, after that first near-disaster with *Take the Money,* was that there was so much still to learn.

With sense, he's loaded

Unless one takes seriously his confession that he prefers dousing himself with talcum powder to taking a shower, the greatest revelation of Woody's expanding universe, as the world turned the corner into the Seventies, was his musical ability.

Two years previously, while playing in *Sam* in San Francisco, a jazzband leader with the engaging name of Turk Murphy had persuaded him to sit in at Earthquake McGoon's, a celebrated haunt of the city's Dixieland disciples. Woody's performance was rated above average for a guy whose practising was limited to time left over from writing hit plays, films of his plays, articles, and stand-up comedy routines. Murphy advised him to 'keep practising'; advice which Woody took so much to heart that he began a habit which is still with him today: he takes his clarinet with him everywhere, blowing for at least an hour or two every day whatever else is on the agenda.

His love of the instrument, he explains, has been with him for twenty years. Since, in fact, an early recording of Sidney Bechet had inspired him, followed by the playing of virtuoso George Lewis. 'In New Orleans,' he said in what, for him, was almost a boastful aside, 'they let me play in a street parade.'

The parade was enlivened by the music of Percy Humphrey's band. Woody also got to play in Congo Square with such instrumentalists of note as Punch Miller, Cie Frazier and Chester Zardis. Never one to let such laurels gather dust, this inspired him to make a major decision: he formed his own jazz band, the New Orleans Funeral and Ragtime

Orchestra.

Sidemen included a working Wall Street stockbroker, John Bucher, on cornet; a teacher (somewhat pompously listed as 'educator'), Dick Dreiwitz on slide trombone; no doubt his wife, Barbara Dreiwitz, studying for a Master's degree in Music, on tuba; an English teacher from Brooklyn College, Dick Miller, on piano; a radio store assistant from Montclair, New Jersey (press agent Richard O'Brien's hometown) named Jay Duke on drums; and a man who was then head writer for the Dick Cavett show on television, and who was to have a long and influential association as a writer with Woody on his major films of the Seventies (*Sleeper, Annie Hall,* and *Manhattan*), ex-country singer Marshall Brickman. Brickman played banjo.

In the icy spring of 1971 the band gathered at Art d'Lugoff's Village Gate to give a concert in aid of the Garden's Nursery School Kindergarten. Tickets at six dollars included a drink. Woody led, and guest star was Eric Knight playing the moog synthesiser. Anyone owning an amateur recording of that show has a collector's piece of considerable rarity, because Woody was too busy to put it on professional tape or disc.

It reflects his respect for jazz, and modest opinion of his own talents as a musician, that he has never attempted to commercialise any of his concerts or live performances (other than the very considerable but unavoidable rise in profits for Michael's Pub in Manhattan, where he sits in on any Monday that the mood and his movements allow).

He has made five recordings of his comedy, routines, some of them hilariously funny, all of them bestsellers. Yet in music, which has a special place in his regard, he remains an obstinate amateur, telling *Newsday* music critic Bob Micklin (while his Barney Googles line-up were entertaining the cognoscenti at Weston's on New York's East Side) 'If I could earn my living as a musician, it would be great. But I don't think I could.'

Underlining this self-effacement was a typical aside to Mark Rosin, who wrote a profile of Woody published in

Harper's magazine later that year, 1971: 'I'm an imperfectionist.' If that is what he is, there are many perfectionists who would like to possess half his capabilities.

Not only had *Take the Money and Run* opened in a New York cinema in August '69, but the same year, while he was playing in *Sam* on Broadway, Woody's film of *Don't Drink the Water* starring one of America's most delightful stage and screen actresses, Estelle Parsons, had earned pleasing reviews. 'An entertaining film – and with a clean B-rating yet!' extolled Frances Herridge in the *New York Post*. By the following June, Woody was already shooting his next movie, *Bananas* (also scripted with Mickey Rose), in Puerto Rico. It opened in April '71 at New York's Coronet cinema. The media was quick to notice that Louise Lasser, reportedly separated from Woody for two years, had been given a leading part.

By now Louise was reduced to doing commercials for a cold-cure and playing the lead in a popular soap-opera on television. In interviews she professed nothing but liking for her ex-husband, claiming that some of her own domestic drawbacks – 'In reality I was the worst wife imaginable,' – had been as much to blame for the break-up as anything he did. She had, she admitted, noticed his continued denigration of marriage in his act, but felt that in her case they were more than justified. She took them in good part, which without any intended pun was what she got in return: Woody cast her again with Lynn Redgrave, Burt Reynolds and a host of other star names in his newest (and to some minds wettest) film, *Everything You Always Wanted to Know About Sex (But Were Afraid To Ask)*.

It opened in August 1972 three months after Woody's first book of collected short pieces, *Getting Even*, was published to launch him yet again as a phenomenal success, this time as a bestselling author. At the last count six years ago, by writer Eric Lax, it had sold 30,000 copies, and ten times that number in paperback. When his second book, *Without Feathers*, appeared in paperback in 1976, it had already been on the *New York Times* bestseller list for four months. His third book, *Side Effects* was published in 1980 and seems set for at least as great a triumph.

In Britain, New English Library paid $50,000 for UK and British Commonwealth rights alone.

Harlene, meanwhile, was reportedly living downtown on West 11th Street, her telephone disconnected. It seems she did not blame herself as Louise did. Nor, it is fairly certain, can she have enjoyed hearing Woody's records, which contained acidulous references to marriage, played over. While Woody and Diane, who had remained 'good friends' after deciding that they no longer wanted to live together as apartment-sharing lovers, were daily publicised as working and living full, rich and varied lives, she must have been working at her easel; regretting, no doubt, the wasted years.

Told of Harlene's suit to claim a million dollars in damages from her son, Mrs Konigsberg was reported to have advised Woody to 'settle for half'. She, at least, appreciated that some of the barbs which came so lightly to Woody's creative tongue were less than kind to his ex-wife. And Harlene's parents, the Rosens of Brooklyn, could never have deserved such things being said, *that* Nettie could be sure of.

Woody was becoming aware that his restless quest for the ideal mate could be expensive in time as well as cash. His divorce from Louise was a friendly affair, but needed the usual amount of concern and professional handling, all of which consumed his energies. As the daughter of a wealthy and prominent man in no way embittered by the severance, Louise could afford to let him off as lightly as was reasonably possible. But attorneys like to earn their bread.

The result was a drag on Woody at a time when he wanted, above all, to be free to write, direct and act. Diane was his least replaceable lady friend. She was too personally elusive and unsure of herself to be tied in marriage to a man who, as she rightly sensed, felt even less self-confidence than herself.

In the eyes of a young New York girl who saw them both from an unusually privileged viewpoint during the year

Woody played in *Sam*, Diane was still in love with him. Linda Hersch was seventeen at the time, a chestnut-haired, vivacious High School senior from the Queens district of Long Island. As president of Woody's first fan club she was allowed unusually intimate glimpses of the pair. She looks back on it now almost with nostalgia, certainly with a warmth of remembered pleasure and excitement. She and ten classmates had intended to form a club to support the actor chosen by Woody to play the Humphrey Bogart character in *Play It Again Sam*, Jerry Lacey. 'He was in a soap (-opera) we all liked called *Dark Shadows*,' she recalls, 'and I went to meet him.'

But Lacey had to tell his daring young visitor that he already had a fan club. 'Why don't you try Woody Allen?' he suggested.

Linda says: 'It seemed like a great idea, though I was sure he'd already have one as well. He didn't though. I went to see him at the theatre where he was playing. We got pictures of him and saw the show.'

To Linda's surprise Woody seemed actually to enjoy having the girls organise themselves as his accredited fans. Everything they had read about his need for privacy, his shyness and his distaste for the ordinary forms of publicity had suggested otherwise. But after they had been his guests at the play several times – given *carte blanche* right to unpaid seats whenever available – he relaxed totally in his dressing room backstage.

'He got so that he'd often change in front of us, right down to his underwear,' she says now, laughing at the recollection. 'Diane was usually there and it was obvious how fond they were of each other. They'd hold hands a lot. Actually, I'm not sure if they were living together then or not, but I could see she adored him. And everything funny he said made her laugh.'

Woody seems to have enjoyed flirting with his adoring young fans nonetheless. 'When I told him how old I was,' Linda remembers, 'he used to kid me about it, telling me "You must be careful with me! Didn't you know my first wife was only seventeen when I married her?" Everyone

143

ribbed us, of course. "When's Woody going to marry you?" – that sort of thing. And his friend Dick Cavett was the worst.'

Cavett was seeing a lot of Woody. They spent bachelor-style days and nights together in various parts of the United States, recalled in some of Cavett's illuminating television interviews with Woody. He enjoyed the girl fans almost as much as Woody did.

'But Diane was so obviously the only woman Woody thought about seriously,' Linda says. 'We were too young, and he didn't really flirt with us, or anything. Once, he did give me a kiss on the cheek, just a friendly little hug and a peck. To tell the truth I was in awe of him most of the time. There was something a bit scary about him to me at that age, though he was always very courteous and nice; very considerate even.' She thinks for a moment. 'Actually, he could be quite stand-offish and rigid sometimes. Kind of strict and not at all emotional, like at other times. I guess only Diane got through to him then, and we used to keep our visits as short as possible.'

Linda has since learned that stars, like comedians, are not always what they project themselves before audiences. She is an editor of a fan magazine in New York reflecting the artificially everyday world of soap-operas and those who play in them (like her original hero, Lacey). Not unnaturally, her consuming desire as Woody's first fan club *supremo* was to please and flatter him.

'I had this idea to give him a surprise birthday party,' she says, smiling a little shyly still at the notion of anything as sweet and simple appealing to Woody Allen, the burnished sophisticate. Linda has a nice dimple in her lower right cheek when she smiles. It's not difficult to see why Woody pretended delight at the occasion – even if he didn't feel it.

'We all brought cakes and presents and things,' Linda says, 'and we just burst in on him and Diane in a flurry of "happy birthdays". I remember it was a bitterly cold day – we held the party on the Saturday before Woody's actual thirty-third birthday on December 1st – I guess it must have been November 29, 1969 – we were all so glad to be inside in

144

his nice warm dressing room. But I really wondered if he'd be pleased to see us.'

She pauses. Her eyes wide with the wonder of that moment. A fan club president at her most magnificent. 'It was all right at first,' she recalls. 'He loved it. But then I produced my *big* surprise, which I'd had to work hard to get ready for him. It was a tape recording of the theme song from *What's New, Pussycat*? I'd brought a player along so that I could surprise him with it.'

The eyes cloud over at the disappointing recollection. 'When he heard what it was,' Linda says, 'he put his hands over his ears. "Shut that thing off!" he begged me. "I don't want to be reminded of that picture. Ever!"'

After that, as Linda sadly admits, 'everything fell a bit flat'.

Woody was aware he'd put a damper on the girls' well-meant birthday party. 'He realised, I think, that he'd spoiled my surprise,' she says. 'Because he suddenly announced that he'd got a surprise for me – a very special present. And he handed me a faded little book.'

The book was *For Auld Lang Syne – A Gift From a Friend to a Friend*. Inside was a pressed piece of brown fern, which may have been plastic, and a rather tatty brown card.

Written on it in Diane Keaton's sprawling handwriting was 'I guess I want to thank you for all the good times. *All* of them.' The line she had drawn under the second 'all' was heavy enough to make it very clear she meant it in the widest possible sense. She had signed it, simply 'Diane'.

Linda read the inscription and could hardly believe her eyes. 'Diane,' she says, 'was right there in the room with us. It seemed incredible to me that he could be giving away something so very personal and intimate to them both. I asked him: "Do you really mean me to have this, Woody?" He didn't answer right away, and I burbled something like "I mean, didn't Diane give it to you specially?" Then, seeing how they both looked I felt really stupid. But Woody reassured me: "No, that's okay," he told me. "You take it." '

It occurred to Linda afterwards that Woody had shown

no sense of loss. 'He didn't seem a bit interested in the fact that he was asking me to accept something Diane must have given him with real feeling,' she says. 'When I got the book home and read some of the loving, sentimental poems inside – including Tennyson's 'I find no place that does not breed some gracious memory of my friend' – it did make me wonder if perhaps their romance was coming to an end. Or already had.'

She had opened the little volume, decorated with pink, bell-like wild flowers, to find another inscription from Diane on the title page. This one was scrawled under a five-pointed star. It read: 'To Woody – Well, you know, you just don't find beautiful books like this any more. I find the introduction especially meaningful.'

Linda says: 'Seeing that the book was published in 1911 it didn't surprise me to find that the introduction was a page and a half of old-fashioned homily on the subject of friendship. But when I read that, and tried to imagine how it would have seemed to any girl in love with the man she was giving it to, it seemed all the more astonishing that Woody had given me the book.'

Before she'd left him that night of the birthday party, Linda had again asked: 'Woody, are you sure you want me to have it?' She remembers: 'He looked a little sheepish then, but he just said: "Go on. Take it." '

Linda took it and treasures both it and the memory of the year when she was as close to Woody as any outsider is ever likely to get. 'He basically shared nothing with us but his time, but that made us happy for a whole year while he was in the play, before he left and Bob Denver took over his role,' she says. 'We all got a terrific high from just being with him.'

Woody gave presents to the other girls as well, impromptu though they almost certainly were, since he had had no forewarning of their celebration. 'One got a huge deco-art, plastic bagel,' Linda remembers, laughing. 'Another of my friends wanted him to let her have his hot-pink sneakers, but Woody wouldn't part with those. We all went home feeling absolutely fabulous. Being then only about fifteen or sixteen at most, that was a real high-light in our lives!'

There were other times when, as part of Woody's personal entourage, Linda and the girls enjoyed privileged close-ups of Woody's world. As his film *Bananas* opened, his admiring friend Cavett hosted a show on television in which he interviewed Woody at length. The girls watched the recording from a studio balcony.

'I'd managed to get a plastic banana,' Linda chuckles. 'Dick Cavett was always pulling our legs, so I decided to get my own back. I threw it down on the stage right in the middle of his interview. Just as he said the title of the film!'

Everybody on the set broke up laughing, of course. Cavett had to run the recording again – only he insisted on keeping the banana, as if it really had come from a fan of Woody's.' 'That' says Linda, 'made me feel really proud.'

Afterwards, Cavett came to Linda's rescue when she was trying to take a flashlight photograph of Woody and him together on stage. Her flash refused to go off. 'He came down, made me take his place with Woody, and managed to get the thing to work,' she recalls gratefully. 'It wasn't a wonderful shot, but a great souvenir all the same.' Linda knew very well how few people were ever permitted to share a snap with Woody, outside those acting with him.

Did she find him attractive? Linda winces slightly at the question. 'How many times have I been asked that?' she says. 'Well, Diane Keaton seemed to think so. She seemed very happy with him, though I'm bound to say I found it strange that they had this thing going between them.'

She pauses, then continues thoughtfully: 'They are such different types. From, I would say, totally different worlds. I thought she was beautiful and wonderful and all that, but very, very spacey sometimes. Only when she talked about theatre and the roles she'd played was she serious and down to earth.'

Diane was appearing on the Johnny Carson television show, with Woody's introduction to help her along. Linda could never quite make out if she was more interested in Woody professionally than in his private self. 'How deeply they felt for each other, or whether they ever talked about marriage, I never really got to know or hear about,' she explains. 'It shocked me when he gave me her book, that I do know. But if it meant they were no longer as close as they had been, I couldn't say.'

At that time, as Linda well remembers, Woody's fans were not nearly so pressing as those he has portrayed with disgust and contempt in his recent film *Stardust Memories*. Linda says: 'We were something else for him at that time. I think he enjoyed seeing us because there weren't too many girls trying to get near him. The only people who came backstage were mostly middle-aged women asking for an autograph. He used to laugh a lot and I believe we seemed funny to him, which we probably were.'

But when *Stardust* came to Queens Linda, who had heard of Woody's harsh fan caricature in the film, went along anxiously to see it. 'I wanted to see if he had made any of the fans in the movie look anything like us,' she says. 'He hadn't, and I'm grateful.'

For that, and for the many kindnesses he showed to Linda and her young friends, she'll never forget the nice side of Woody. Not to mention the gift of a small, faded book inscribed with a message from Diane's heart at its fullest. There are few in Woody's entourage who have been so generously rewarded.

Jack Hirschberg, one of Hollywood's most experienced press and publicity executives (recently on the award winning *Ordinary People* film), also shared aspects of Woody's life during the time of his affaire with Diane. Like fan club presidents, a major press agent must be given privileged views of his star if he is to make anything of the assignment to promote his subject most widely. For Jack, publicity director for Woody's film *Play It Again Sam*, the limits put on him were not always acceptable.

As he frankly says: 'Woody is a very complicated character. I got along with him okay, but it took an effort.'

Knowing that Woody was both neurotic and inexperienced affected Hirschberg in two ways: he wanted to help an obviously talented writer overcome his shyness with the press and media while coping with a new and wider form of exposure; and he was faced with the problem of projecting a hitherto 'cult' figure onto the wider canvas of general acceptability and popularity.

Neither proved easy. Jack Hirschberg reflects sadly: 'I'd say he did *most* of what I asked him to do. That's to say, while the picture was on the floor, being made. After that I can't say the same.'

For this, the seventh film Woody had been involved in, he had – in Hirschberg's opinion, wisely – allowed the talented Herbert Ross to relieve him of the burden of direct-ing. 'He needed a firm hand, and Herb Ross provided it,' says Hirschberg. 'Woody, I firmly believe, stood in great need of that controlling influence at that time.' He adds: 'He's brilliant in a lot of ways, but he still had a tremendous lot to learn about direction. And in presenting himself to the public, too, I'd say.'

A rueful Jack Hirschberg used all his talents and powers of persuasion to try to project Woody's controversial image. 'He kept telling me he was only popular with a small, select band of fans,' he recalls. 'I had to try to make him see that this film could bring him much wider atten-tion. *Sam*, I'm sure, was the best picture he could possibly have made at that time. He'd written it as a play, which had been a big hit in New York. All it needed was for its appeal, or rather *his* appeal, to be broadened for world cinema audiences to make him a major attraction. That was my problem. Because, unfortunately, he proved less than co-operative about it sometimes.'

Hirschberg still wonders if it was Woody's shyness, or a misunderstanding, which caused him to let down one of his best contacts, a leading journalist. He explains: 'I believed Woody had given me his word more than once, that he'd write me a signed piece on how he wrote the play. I'd promised this. But I never got it, and I still don't know why not.'

He doesn't believe this was wilful neglect on Woody's part. But, professionally, it hurt. 'Let me say,' Jack Hirschberg says apologetically, 'I think he's one of the most brilliant minds I've ever worked with. Fresh ideas pour out of him. And, once he grows to trust you, he becomes a lot easier to work with, though I'm bound to qualify that: he never was *easy* to work with.'

Yet Woody could delight certain writers and journalists who happened to get to him at the right moment, and were able to set him talking about himself and his work. Hirschberg found that bringing pressmen to meet him on these occasions was a joy. But there were other times, rather more of them, when nothing fizzed.

'He gave very few interviews,' Hirschberg says. 'And they weren't always what the journalists and editors wanted. He was, I had to accept the "thinking man's writer". And an intensely private individual.'

In spite of the privileged intimacy his role on the picture gave him, Hirschberg seldom glimpsed Woody's personal life. He kept his friends and emotions curtained off. 'I never knew how it was,' Hirschberg admits. 'He had this very close relationship going with Diane Keaton, and I got to know her, of course. But I never really understood even that.'

To Jack Hirschberg, well versed in the strange needs of Hollywood stars and celebrities, the romance between Woody and Diane was an enigma. 'They are entirely different people,' he explains, 'emotionally and in every other way possible. For instance, she is far more "up" than he is, much livelier and more effervescent. He's a serious man off the set, doesn't crack jokes or horse around like Jerry Lewis, for instance: jumping on tables and making an ass of himself. Not Woody.'

So the mystery of what attracted Woody Allen to Diane Keaton was one which not only a wondering outside world pondered, but also one of filmland's most experienced technicians.

In Hirschberg's opinion, it was largely their shared devotion to cinema. Woody had always revelled in films, telling everyone who would listen in his early days how he had devoured them as a boy, and since. Diane was a budding, dedicated actress of tremendous potential. Yet what she

150

had to offer might never have been recognised but for Woody. It flowered under Woody's appreciative hand, where previously it had been all but ignored.

As Jack Hirschberg rightly says: 'He really made it bloom. He showcased it. In *Sam*, where she played Linda to his Allan Felix, if you remember, he favoured her whenever it was possible. So, of course he helped her with her career, though I'm not saying that was the only reason she liked him. They really did show great mutual affection.'

Nor is Jack Hirschberg bearing the slightest grudge over Woody's painful reluctance to be interviewed as widely, and as often, as the press director would have wished. 'He was never nasty to me,' Hirschberg says. 'His only fault in my eyes, if it is a fault, is that he was just too reticent. That's what he was.'

That's what he still is, as opera singer Shirley Potter from St Louis will never lightly forget. She tells the story of her encounter with Woody on the sidewalks of New York, even though it gets a laugh at her expense.

'It was in the late Seventies,' she tells friends. 'I recognised Woody on the street. Just walking along between Second and Third Avenues.' Shirley knew, of course, that Woody Allen likes to remain incognito. 'So it seemed it would be a lot of fun to talk to him,' she says.

And in midtown Manhattan, everyone talks to everyone else. Celebrities usually pass unnoticed among the crowds. Only those like Greta Garbo or Elliott Gould (and Woody Allen) find any need to wear disguises and dodge their fans. So Shirley didn't think he could possibly mind a few cordial words.

'I went up and said "Hi! Woody Allen, would you mind if I walked over a couple of blocks with you?" He just smiled. He didn't answer.

'It was weird. I laughed, I think, to cover my embarrassment. Then I said something like "Well I won't try to sell you anything. Or even talk to you if you don't want to talk."'

At which Woody did open his mouth. Shirley says: 'He said: "Go right ahead." And so we walked along maybe three or four blocks in total silence! He never said one word. I was beginning to feel really stupid. Imagine, here I was pacing it out with this mature guy, someone I may probably have had a whole lot in common with if he'd cared to open his mouth, and he was staying absolutely dumb!'

When this thought got to her, Shirley Potter began to feel even more stupid than before. At the next corner she announced: 'Well, this is where I have to turn off.' Woody hardly seemed disappointed. As Shirley says: 'I probably also said something idiotic like thanking him for letting me walk along beside him, breathing the same air. Anyway, when I told him I was quitting he actually smiled.

' "Pity," he told me. "If you'd stayed with me another couple of blocks, to where I'm due to meet with Elliott Gould, you could have walked in silence with him as well!" I guess he enjoyed the joke, even if I didn't.'

After such an uninformative encounter, Shirley Potter would not be expected to realise that enjoying his own humour is seldom within Woody's grasp. Marshall Brickman is not the only collaborator who has described Woody (in his case to the widest possible American public, on a Dick Cavett televised interview in June 1978) as 'not a lot of laughs'.

'To walk on the street with him, people think must be hilarious,' Brickman told Cavett (who already knew this only too well). 'Not so. Woody is a very serious person, though only his intimates see that.'

The intimates include his managers and close friends; Diane Keaton, Tony Roberts, Jean Doumanian, Mickey Rose and a handful of others. Even they were surprised when Woody finally decided to put his cap and bells aside, in his first all-serious film, *Interiors*. Kafka's clown, out there on his own again, risking his neck.

Plain talk, he's crazy

Whether the risk was worth taking is not a question Woody Allen cares to consider. It has always been his contention that he would have been happier as someone else – a baseball star perhaps, or an intellectual egghead. A similar impatience stamps his refusal to type himself in his choice of subjects.

Nevertheless, *Interiors* was more than simply a shift in direction; there wasn't a laugh in it. To many of Woody's most devoted, normally tolerant fans it came as something of an electrified culture shock.

Wisely, its creator had avoided taking part in it himself. Woody directed his story (of a middle-aged, tragically deserted wife and mother driven to suicide) with total involvement, but he recognised the impossibility of his clown playing Hamlet. It was enough that this script, which seemed to have been torn from some hidden part of his psyche, should be brought to the screen; whether or not it astonished and dismayed many who paid to see it never worried him for a moment.

Woody Allen, one felt, was warning us not to take his comedy for granted. But whatever reason he may have had for making this apple-pie bed of a movie, had it failed in its own right as an intensely moving human drama he would have found it hard to get back even to his well-tried humour roles.

In fact, *Interiors* was a masterpiece. *Variety* placed it among the best ten films of 1978. The British journal *Films and Filming* heralded it as the best feature film 'from any source'.

It was also his first unbridled attempt at what he likes to call 'grown up' workmanship in the cinema. For years, since recovering from the juvenile infatuation of the Brooklyn Theatre days when almost anything that moved, jumped and threw custard pies on the screen delighted him, Woody had been entranced by the cinematic art and dramatic purity of directors Ingmar Bergman, Sergei Eisenstein, Federico Fellini, Michelangelo Antonioni and Bernardo Bertolucci. Fellini's $8\frac{1}{2}$ transfixed him the moment he saw its powerful images float onto the screen. From his first introduction to the serious cinema he had harboured a nagging urge to emulate such directors.

Until *Interiors,* there had been little opportunity to do anything of the sort. However sympathetic his backers were to his demands, there were limits to their willingness to indulge fancies. Deserting the sure and successful for the untried was bad business. It was only after *Annie Hall* had given them the assurance of a box-office winner that they let him have his head.

Much of the credit for this must go to Jack Rollins and Charley Joffe. After *Pussycat* in 1965, it had taken Joffe eighteen hard-slogging months to set up a deal for their still unknown writer-actor and would-be director. United Artists, until *Pussycat's* takings were in, refused to back him. Only after the still limited successes of *Tiger Lily* in 1966, *Casino Royale* in 1967, and *Don't Drink the Water* in 1969 (in none of which Woody played more than an insignificant role) would they consider him a valuable asset. The success of these early pictures gave them, as Lee Guthrie says, 'second thoughts'. The writer explains: 'Joffe was able to negotiate a contract rather quickly with David Picker, then president of United Artists. Its terms were: two million dollars budget per film, total control for Woody once UA had approved the story idea, and a three-picture deal.'

Still, looking back, it's not hard to see how grudging this contract was, and how much it depended for its continuation (being subject, as always to any number of small-print clauses which could prevent, or indefinitely hold up, each successive picture) entirely on Woody's ability to bring home the bacon. Joffe had fought long and hard to win the deal from the Hollywood company, but even he knew that the odds against Woody making an uninterrupted flow of three successful, money-making films were precarious.

Woody, though, showed a sublime indifference to such fears. While it's clear that he was learning to walk before attempting to run, there is no suggestion that he felt hampered by the weight of responsibility. Having two million dollars to play with on each of his scripts didn't bother him. The result, as we know, was that he made money with all three.

The first was *Bananas*. This was released in 1971. Then came *Everything You Want to Know About Sex (But Were Afraid To Ask)* in 1972. And finally *Sleeper*, in 1973.

Meanwhile, the small company Charley Joffe had persuaded to put up money for Woody's rewritten stage play *Play It Again, Sam* (Palomar Pictures) released the film in 1972. All four of these first films of Woody's turned in a profit. When totted up, it came to ten and a half million dollars – at a cost of only eight and three quarters.

Sam, the one film UA had been too cautious to back, had contributed over eleven million dollars by itself. The studio had had to learn by its costly mistake. And Woody's signature – guided by an exultant Charley Joffe – was quickly added to a new, four-picture contract with United Artists on even better and more independent terms.

Under this, he made *Love and Death*, released in 1975, and followed it with *Annie Hall* in 1977. The studio felt, no doubt, that he could do no wrong. So *Interiors* went ahead, whatever their misgivings on its score. Even Hollywood allows certain indulgencies for good box-office conduct.

And in its way *Interiors* has been an important advance for Woody and UA combined. It has not lost money. And in terms of cinema values it has introduced Woody's work to a wider and more discriminating audience. It's release in 1978, soon after the extremely valuable success of *Annie Hall*, was triumphantly followed the next year, 1979, by Woody's *Manhattan*. Whatever the critics thought of this sophisticated comedy of a man torn between love for a teenage girl and somebody his own age, it did nothing to diminish Woody's universal and spreading appeal.

Also, Woody had made an interesting departure while all this was going on. In principle, he refuses to work with other writers' material, or to take part as an actor in films he has not written. *The Front*, in 1976, was the exception. And the reason may well have been that Woody felt a serious call on his personal and political conscience.

The Front was intended to be a lighthearted but telling exposition of the McCarthy reign-of-terror in which many Hollywood scriptwriters and directors were blacklisted for their left-wing associations, however remote. Woody took part out of sympathy with the ideals of those making and playing in it, some of whom had been victims of the purge. Sadly, the film failed to make its point with conviction or to justify the faith of those who, like Woody, had given it their support.

But it was by no means his worst performance. Under direction, Woody is often less self-conscious than in his own films. Under Herb Ross in *Sam* he also flowered. *The Front*, made for Columbia and directed by Martin Pit, gave Woody's acting talent full reign.

As a director, he has learned a great deal since *Take the Money*. After another go at direction, with *Bananas*, he recognised the need for a reflective break, which was why he invited Ross to take over the helm with *Play it Again, Sam*. There are those who believe that this competent director's versatile techniques have helped Woody to achieve far greater confidence and distinction.

Whether this is so or not, Woody returned to the chair to direct his spoof of perversion and fornication in *Sex*. Since then, he has handled each of his subsequent pictures with growing assurance and skill. Today, Woody Allen is seriously considered to be one of, if not the greatest of all, the most talented American directors working.

Simultaneously, the actor in him has been unconsciously developing its public image. This is as the sexual loser, who sweeps off the board – and the broad – before the end credit titles come up. The subtlest of his many talents is unquestionably that, whereas Chaplin won the lady's heart by making her view him through a blur of tears, Woody pulls them into his arms like a veritable Galahad. He actually *wins* the affection of such superbly beautiful women as Diane Keaton and Charlotte Rampling, and does so credibly. We believe it. Also we know by virtue of his unrestrained public admissions (the one personal subject he is *not* shy about) that in real life, too, he has had more than his share of conquests. It all adds to his quite extraordinary image as the Great Screen Lover.

Mel Karman put it to him bluntly: 'Is it a burden being an intellectual sex symbol?' It was a question, as he explained, which he had asked Paul Newman. Woody, in Karman's words, let 'a thoughtful pause' fall between them. Then asked: 'What did *he* say?'

Karman told him: 'That he didn't think he was. That it was all a hyped-up myth.'

Woody, always the diffident violet in interviews where he is not indulging in outrageous leg-pulling, nodded.

'Right,' he said. 'Well, that goes double for me.'

True? One begs leave to doubt that, since the most endearing planks in his screen platform are the handicaps he was born with (small, Jewish, impoverished) and the success he has achieved in spite of them. It is their design which runs through his work like a silver thread. The myth of Woody, pre-destined loser, overcoming harsh fate to triumph, eventually, in love is its hallmark.

Often, as in *Stardust Memories*, it takes strange forms. Yet basically it is always there, underlying every plot. We, of course, see it as screamingly funny – that is, those of us who accept that he is the greatest comic of the age. But while we're laughing, he is getting into bed with wonderful women like Diane Keaton who appear to dote on his somewhat hard-to-define charms.

Not quite everyone finds this easy to believe.

'Woody Allen? You gotta be kidding. I wouldn't dance with *him* . . .' an eighteen-year-old Brooklyn disco girl is quoted as saying in *New York Post* reporter Stephen Silverman's book *Public Spectacles* (Dutton, 1981). Frank as this is,

157

it tells us only that some girls do *not* see Woody as a sex symbol.

Truly astonishing is the number who do, as a New York psychiatrist has recently revealed. This young woman, Dr Dee Burton, is herself an attractive, dark-haired beauty. Her motivation for becoming interested in Woody's lady-killer propensities began ten years ago when she had a dream about him.

Dr Burton decided many years later, following a dinner party where others confessed to having had the same experience, to search around for as many people as she could find who had suffered, or enjoyed, the nocturnal fantasy of a visitation from Woody. To her complete surprise: 'I found scores of people in New York and Los Angeles – the only two cities I researched in – who'd had dreams, all kinds of dreams, but mostly favourable, about or involving Woody Allen.'

The reason why he percolates into these areas of the subconscious (usually more inclined to reflect the Robert Redfords and Jane Fondas of the age) has a lot to do with our individual identification with him, Dr Burton says.

'The desire to achieve what he achieves, to emulate his surprising success, is at the root of most of the dreams I came across,' she explains. To Dee Burton, Woody in his early films always seemed 'a very awkward person, having difficulty with the opposite sex.' So that many of the dreamers apparently gain a feeling of self-acceptance from seeing someone else – someone respected, rich and famous – presenting himself in this way.

They also, she believes, deeply admire an essential quality of Woody's work, its artistic integrity. 'This comes across again and again,' Dr Burton says. 'It reflects his own kind of genuineness. They see that he doesn't make movies to pander to popular taste. That he won't accept censorship. And that he seems to be saying something all the time that he truly believes in.'

To that extent, Dr Burton believes, the dreamers and many who feel the same way but don't project their fantasies in sleep, identify with Woody's native sensibility. It

158

only fails to move them when his most practised image (the poor little Jewish guy from Coney Island, undersized, undernourished, but still reaching out for the supreme goals of sexual fulfilment and mastery of beautiful women) slips.

'There are doubters,' she admits. 'One dreamer I met had been in a cinema with Woody, watching one of his films. The dream suggested that Woody didn't want anyone to know he was there, so that he could observe their reaction impersonally. But what happened was he deliberately let himself be recognised, got chased out of the cinema by clutching fans (like in *Stardust Memories*), then turned to his companion and said: "See what I mean? I can't go anywhere without this happening!" '

She laughs at the recollection. 'I think that was really delightful,' she says. 'But of course there are contradictions in his life now. You can't be driven around in a white Rolls Royce and throw parties for hundreds of the world's most glamorous people without attracting attention.'

In the same way many of Dr Burton's dreamers felt betrayed by *Stardust*, because of its hostility towards fans they took to be Woody's – a fact he strenuously denies. 'I heard a lot of negative comments about that,' Dr Burton comments. 'Even more than about the Rolls and eating at smart, expensive restaurants and so forth. And then I've certainly had people, particularly Jewish people, feeling very defensive about his treatment of women.'

These critics are very often strongly feminist. Lee Guthrie is not Jewish, but this Southern American writer who now lives in New York once studied Woody for her abortive (he suppressed it in a 1978 legal action) book on him. She has strong feelings about his ascendant male chauvinism.

'This is not a man who relates to adult women,' she says. 'He is six weeks older than I am, but I can't imagine having an affair with a seventeen-year-old boy from Dalton (a US university). On any level, I can't imagine it. That's what Allen does in *Manhattan* with a girl of that age. He's nymphet-related.'

159

Guthrie backs her belief that Woody is 'sexist; against women', with telling observations of his other films. 'The way the ex-wife was presented in *Annie Hall*,' she says. 'That is a perfect example. A cold intellectual bitch. And Annie, the girl, was a child; a twittish infant really. There's something wrong when you see women presented in this way.'

Lee is talking to Virginia Field, film art director. 'I'd never thought of it like that,' Virginia agrees. 'I love Woody, but that's right. He does show women up in that way. I can't deny it.'

Lee adds, 'Whenever I find men who are only comfortable around child-girls and child-women it makes clicks go off in my head. This older-man-younger-women relationship is a sexist staple in our culture, but there's just something about it that puts me off. All right, Woody made it okay for the American male to be inadequate. All those beautiful young women he gets! No looks, but that's okay too. You can get yourself laid in a gorgeous Fifth Avenue apartment just like Woody Allen whatever your chest measurement. Even Diane Keaton is within range!'

Allowing for her disappointment over Woody's successful injunction against her book, on the grounds of plagiarising his and another writer's work and misusing his publicity material, Lee Guthrie is making a number of points here which other women find disturbing in Woody's more serious work.

What Charles Chaplin described in his own defence ('. . . ridicule is an attitude of defiance: we must laugh in the face of our helplessness against the forces of nature, or go insane . . .') Woody uses as a blunt instrument to belittle the female sex. He reveals them as erotic playthings, sex-object stereotypes, fundamentally inadequate beings. Only his own complete helplessness saves them from being overshadowed in his major films.

In real life the hang-ups are differently placed but made of much the same material. In *Annie Hall* he describes sex as 'the most fun I've ever had without laughing,' which makes it seem both agreeable and childlike. But his comment afterwards from such a confirmed workaholic suggests

160

Previous page: With a fair-haired Diane Keaton, 1970. (RON GALELLA)
Top: With Diane at a New York reception, 1972. (RON GALELLA)
Bottom: With Diane on the set of his banned political satire. (TONY MARSHALL)
Right: Holding hands with Diane, 1977. (RON GALELLA)

Top: Outside Elaine's with two friends, 1978. (RON GALELLA)
Bottom: With Jean Doumanian, 1980. (DAVID McGOUGH – RETNA LTD)

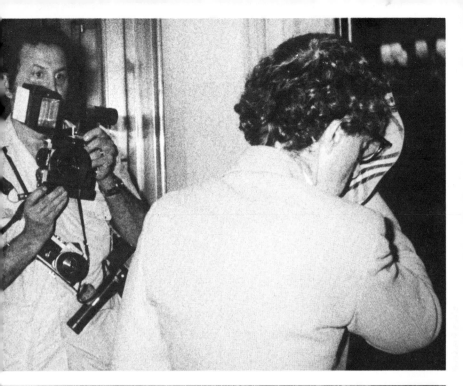

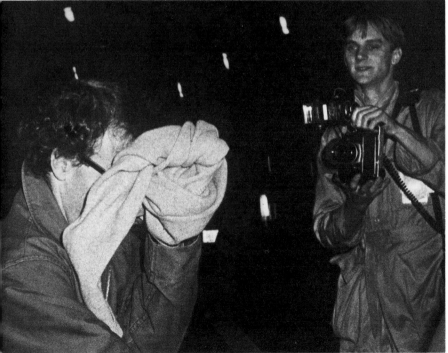

Woody takes cover from paparazzi Ron Galella (above) and avid McGough (below). (RON GALELLA)

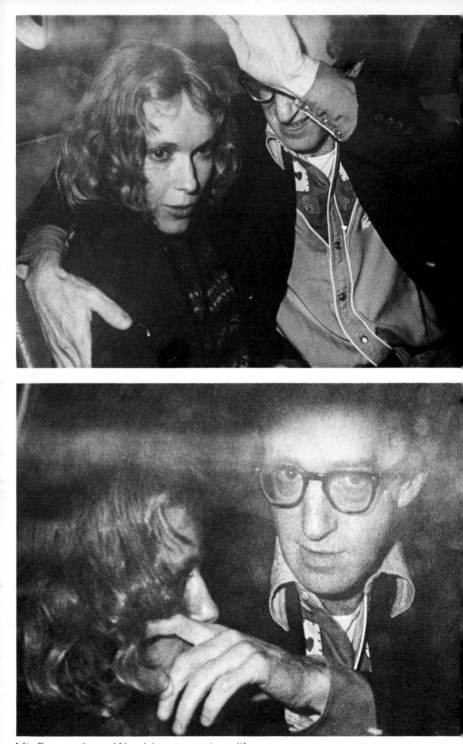
Mia Farrow shares Woody's not-so-private life. (BETTY BURKE GALELLA)

op: Woody and Mia pose peacefully for David McGough in her New ork apartment, 1981. (DAVID McGOUGH – RETNA LTD)

ottom: The menu cannot conceal Woody's reflected image as he dines ith Mia at a New York restaurant, 1981. (DAVID McGOUGH – RETNA LTD)

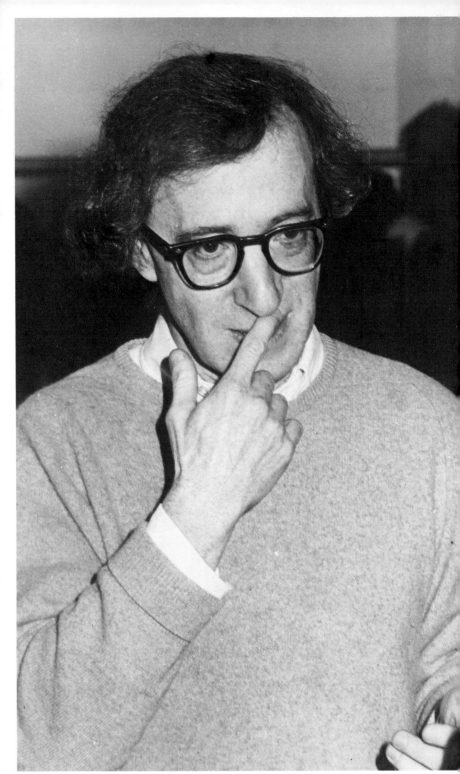

A pensive moment during rehearsals for Woody's 1981
Broadway play *The Floating Light Bulb*. (DAVID McGOUGH – RETNA LTD)

inadequacy. 'As Balzac said,' Woody complains wryly, 'there goes another novel.'

It's almost as if Woody Allen's aesthetic eye sees sex as another painful necessity, like exposing himself to sunlight. At the end of the same picture, he narrates the anecdote of a man who seeks a psychiatrist's advice about his brother. 'He thinks he's a chicken,' he explains. 'You'd better turn him in,' says the doctor. 'I can't,' the man says 'I need the eggs.' As Woody says, in explanation of this old wisecrack: 'That's the trouble with human relationships. They're irrational, crazy, stupid . . . but we need the eggs.'

He also needs, it seems, a strong female arm now and again to guide his awkwardly faltering footsteps. 'Woody can trip over things that aren't even in his way,' says his old schoolfriend Nino Pantano. The woman whose elegant hand seems to do much of the guiding is also an old friend, but not one customarily associated with the Woody Allen inner circle.

Her name is Jean Doumanian. *Post* reporter Stephen Silverman, who knows Doumanian and has been with her in Woody's company, says, 'She helped develop his taste. That apartment in *Stardust Memories* is *very* Jean. Also the advertisements used to promote the film.'

Between them, though, friends say there is not and never has been any romance. They apparently make a truism of the cliché 'We're just good friends.' That and nothing else, though Jean will quip to Silverman: 'Woody has me laughing from the minute we wake up in the morning.' When they do, we may be sure it is in different beds. Jean Doumanian has already suffered one broken marriage, and Silverman swears she has absolutely no intention of becoming the next Mrs Woody Allen.

Woody's more intimate life is rather like the dark side of the moon, in that so few living beings ever get to see, let alone share, it. But Jean is one of the privileged insiders who do. Silverman ventures the opinion that she appreciates the spin-off from Woody's celebrity status. 'To put it mildly,' he says, 'I'd say that her friendship with him sheds a certain light on her. He is a star.'

The fact that their relationship dates back to the early Sixties, when Woody was almost totally unknown, may also suggest that this is not the only thread binding them together. Yet it can't be ruled out. Stephen Silverman, as the *New York Post*'s entertainments editor, sees behind many a scene. In his book detailing the high-stepping life he leads, he tells how he first met Doumanian with Woody and Marshall Brickman. She was then the associate producer of the television show from which she was fired last spring, *Saturday Night Live*. Silverman was informed: 'People usually use Jean to get to Woody.'

If it is at all possible, that would certainly seem to be a sure route. 'Mostly, she's in charge when they're together,' Silverman says. 'She rules the roost, no doubt about it. Drags him off to parties. Even tells him how to dress.' She also gets on well with the Konigsbergs, Woody's mother and father.

Jean Doumanian's remarkable climb up the showbiz and social ladder owes much to Woody. They reportedly met when she was a buyer for three women's specialty shops, or boutiques, in Chicago. Woody and Dick Cavett were on the loose in the city, and meeting Jean, who has no lack of talent, led to her going to work for Cavett, booking celebrities for his show. It led on to an ABC variety series contract on the same lines, finding foils for the star of the show, Howard Cosell. As *TV Guide* writer Sally Bedell has recorded: 'When the Cosell show bombed in 1976, friend Woody helped her land a similar job booking celebrities on NBC's *Saturday Night Live*.' It was certainly no surprise to Silverman when Jean confided to him that she regards Woody as one of the most generous men in her life.

The rest is New York television history, in that Jean Doumanian rose from her routine job in the front office to a $15,000 a week producer slot on the same programme. Nobody wants to say that Woody had a hand in his friend's rapid, not to say phenomenal, ascendancy, but there can't be much doubt that he was pleased. More pleased, apparently, than Lorne Michaels, the show's creator and pro-

162

ducer, who told Sally Bedell she had not been consulted. To Miss Michaels, Jean Doumanian 'had never shown even a glimmer of interest in writing, and comedy was not her strong suit.' Others connected with the show expressed almost equal astonishment.

Doumanian lasted only four months, during which time Woody *was* able to help his friend, materially. For instance, he sent her a girl player named Ann Risley who had had bit parts in three of his latest movies, and recommended her for the show. Jean hired Ann, as she did Woody's sister, Letty Aronson (to write for the show), and a former small-town news reporter called Charles Rocket – reportedly because a woman NBC executive thought he was 'sexy'.

Sally Bedell dug around after Jean was fired in March 1981 and came up with the fact that Woody and Jean had talked 'several times a day' on the telephone to each other about the show and its problems. 'The influence of Allen caused endless speculation,' Sally wrote. Jean replied to all queries from those who wondered with an absolutely frank statement, but no admission. 'We're the best of friends,' she told everybody. 'Of course Woody helps me.'

The trouble seems to have been that it was the wrong sort of help. Sally Bedell says: 'Particularly irksome to critics were the cheap jokes about Jews, drugs and homosexuality.' This could certainly never be levelled as criticism of Woody. His material has been described as many things, but cheap is not an adjective that is ever likely to be applied to it.

Discussing the debacle, a top NBC man said of Jean: 'She tried very hard, but she was in over her head.' For once it seems that the failure of the show to come alive may have been over Woody's head too. His own sister had lost out, as had others he had backed. Letty suffered from the disadvantage of having had no previous professional experience (other than as closet-critic of Woody's work), so that the discredit of seeing her first show fail did little to help her budding career as a researcher. It will be interesting to see if, with his usual generosity to those close to him, Woody offers any further help.

If he does, it will not be unusual. He often stresses the value he places on genuine relationships. His one-time admiring kid sister is still one of his closest and most sincere fans. She finds his humour hilarious, friends say, and listens to Woody's material endlessly when he want an opinion from an outside source. Like Diane Keaton and Louise Lasser, (but not his less fortunate first wife Harlene) Woody stays loyally in touch with all the women he has shared any really profound moments with.

'You know, I love Diane,' he confessed to Karman in 1978. 'We haven't been lovers for many years – not since we lived together five years ago – but we're real close friends. I count myself lucky.'

So, too, does Diane. And Louise Lasser's continuing friendship suggests a similar gratitude. The man who married her, starred her in his films, then divorced her after five years of marriage, still commands her loyal affection. Woody admits to liking only attractive, intelligent, charming women, but he is also capable of devotion to any woman who happens, as they very rarely do, to mesh in with his emotional and physical requirements.

Mia Farrow in 1981 was the obvious complement. Her warm, maternal nature, the experience she had gained of widely differing men, having been married to Frank Sinatra and André Previn, gave her the unspoilt maturity Woody desperately needs. Jack Rollins, very much a family man himself, confesses to being unsure whether Woody knows how fond of children he is; but Gene Siskel got it out of him. 'I have always liked kids,' Woody told him. 'The only reason I've never had any is because I've never had a marriage that has worked. Listen to me – never.'

Woody went on to describe some of the reasons, an unusual declaration suggesting that at the time of the interview (mid-June 1981) he was seriously contemplating the question of issue. Perhaps even a shade bitter that in his forty-sixth year he was still childless. There was more than a hint of sadness as he confessed to Siskel: 'When I was married to Louise I definitely would have had children with her, but we knew early on that we'd better be careful about that because we weren't sure it was going to last . . . But I've been taking out Mia Farrow for the last year, and she has seven children, and it's fine. I enjoy it. It's a treat.'

Gene Siskel pressed home his point. 'If Mia were willing to have children,' he asked, 'would you be willing to have a child with her?'

Woody's reply destroys any suggestion, implicit or assumed, that he has ever had the slightest reluctance to become a father. 'If I was married to her,' he said, 'sure. Oh sure. You know, I've always felt that my attitude about having children was dependent on the woman I was with. If she didn't want children, I could easily not have them. It's not the burning desire of my life, 'cause you always have kids to play with. Your friends have kids. My sister has a niece and nephew who I play with all the time. But if I were married to someone who wanted twelve kids, that would be okay too.'

Who will inspire him to this can only be conjecture. But trends are discernible. For instance, Woody has plainly shown recently an aversion to American women. 'There is not an American lady as beautiful and neurotic as (British) Charlotte Rampling,' he told a German girl interviewer, Viviane Naefe recently. 'Nor one who is so warm, feminine and beautiful as (French) Marie-Christine Barrault.'

One must assume that Mia Farrow, as American as apple pie, knows Woody is not joking when he says this. But she may also know that the distance between Woody's head and heart is infinite.

Go hit your head against the wall

In August 1972 Woody declared himself against censorship. His *Sex* movie had just opened in New York. *Sam* was packing audiences into Radio City Music Hall as it had been for three months, helped by a long-winded review in *Time* magazine by-lined 'Harry Flecks' (but written anonymously by a twenty-two-year-old college boy drop-out who, as the magazine's editor shrewdly realised, was archetypical of Woody's closest fans). 'One walks out,' he wrote, 'feeling a little discouraged: the brilliant comic scenes and lines remind one of the film this could have been – of the great movie comedy Woody Allen may still make one day.'

And which Woody fully intended to make. Not 'one day', but as soon as time would allow. He had, he told Fred Bruning of *Newsday*, turned down offers of further television series 'because of censorship'. He had made a one-hour-long wickedly satirical film on President Richard Nixon (he called him 'Dixon') and Henry Kissinger (Wallinger), the globe-trotting secretary of state, for America's public television channels. When he was forced to accept its cancellation, one can assume in view of his attitude to censorship that this must have rankled with him; far more than he has ever admitted in public. All he has ever said about the incident, which blew up into a scandal hinting at political suppression and secrecy, has been mild in the extreme.

All copies of the film are supposed to have been destroyed by order, but one or two escaped. Seeing one of these cut-down remains of Woody's spoof today, one can only ponder the reason why such a broad and only occasionally funny piece should have aroused interest, let alone political or private ire. It has to be remembered that it was made during the run-up period to Richard Nixon's second-term election. And long before Watergate.

Woody obviously knew that Nixon himself was not above a little clowning. The president had appeared on the widely popular *Laugh In* show on television, using the catch-phrase 'sock it to me' to bring the house down. Could such a man, Woody may well have reasoned, object to a broad lampoon on himself and his secretary of state, Kissinger?

This was the question, in fact, which Jim Day, the then president of New York's Channel 13 TV Station where Woody's film was made and about to be shown, ultimately had to answer. Day, now a professor at Brooklyn College, and able for the first time to talk about this awkward moment in his dedicated career as a public-spirited broadcaster, found himself having to make a decision which could have had disastrous effects.

To kill the film implied a censorship he stoutly resented, even if the reasons for doing so were fundamentally that it was not a very good film. To run it might endanger the public funds which alone provide the United States with advertisement-free television.

As Jim Day now explains, the fears of his senior management colleagues in this connection also played a part in the drama of Woody's little film. They blew it up into a thumping great headache for the station and all concerned; one that deserves a fuller explanation than has ever been given of it.

The facts are these, in Jim Day's recorded words: 'We'd commissioned the programme some time before and the thing had been made for showing. So far as I knew, though I'd never seen it, we were going ahead with it. Then one day the vice president of programmes came to see me in a rather worried frame of mind. He told me he'd read the script and didn't like it. It wasn't funny and he had other objections to it, in view of the political connections.

'Well, I told him that if that was how he felt – and he

167

obviously did feel it, strongly – "we'd better cancel, and eat the cost." That's an expression we use to mean that the thing has to be written off as a dead loss.'

Day continues with his tale. There was more to the cancellation, it seems, than merely the level of entertainment of Woody's script. As the ex-president says:

'The station had recently been in trouble with the press over what *Variety*, the showbusiness magazine, had labelled censorship. We'd cut a line or two from scripts, and they'd got to hear about it. So we were particularly sensitive. But the producer of Woody's show had spent a year making the film and naturally he wanted it shown.'

Professor Day admits that he agreed to further attempts being made to 'get the thing into shape' – resulting in the sixty-minute film being trimmed to less than half its length. He also admits that finally, it was he who killed it. But, by that time a storm had blown up which was threatening more than just Woody's spoof.

'Washington (the PBS main office) telephoned my boss, attorney Ethan Alan Hitchcock, to say that if any one of our 150 to 200 stations around the United States ran the programme "it might well endanger the grant of public funds for public broadcasting." The question I then had to ask myself was; *had I the right to jeopardise the whole financial future of PBS by showing it?*'

There were even closer pressures. As Day says: 'The people at the top of PBS knew almost nothing of Woody, My chairman asked me, when he saw rushes of the show, "Who is that?". Ethan Hitchcock's reaction was entirely based on what he'd heard over the telephone from Washington. They'd told him that John W. Macey Jr, who created the corporation for public broadcasting in 1967, was "apoplectic".'

Whether or not Macey himself had seen the show is doubtful. Certainly neither Day nor his superior Hitchcock had at this stage. 'Ethan phoned me straight away. Had I seen it? he wanted to know. I hadn't. Then, would I do so immediately and let him have my feelings on it?'

Now thoroughly aware of the gravity of it all, Jim Day

168

took the station's attorneys into the theatre with him. 'There was a scene in which the character called Harvey Wallinger, played by Woody and an obvious take off of Henry Kissinger – was described by a nun, licking her lips, as "very sexy!" It was obviously in very bad taste.'

Day told Hitchcock only that there were problems. It was enough. 'Let me see it right away,' Hitchcock requested. As Jim Day recalls it: 'He was calling me over the weekend, about every half hour or so. It had got to be absurd. I decided the time had come to try to get back on the rails, and I wanted to call in the executive committee of the board to make the decision. But Hitchcock kept arguing and saying that wasn't the issue. In his view, *nobody* should see it until I – who had executive responsibility – had decided if it was suitable for showing nationwide during an election campaign.'

For the rest of a very worrying weekend, Day stalled Hitchcock by telling him that first *he* had to see the film himself. Then he would decide. As he says: 'By the time I got to my office on the Monday, Ethan was already in the theatre seeing a screening. When he came out his face was a picture. He said nothing to me. He went straight back to his office in Rockefeller Plaza and within an hour I received a typed memorandum from him saying that *on no account* must the programme be shown.'

Though he takes responsibility for the abandonment of Woody's Harvey Wallinger satire which followed, it was only after Hitchcock's instruction that the order to kill it went out from Jim Day's desk. 'I was disappointed,' he remembers. 'I knew how hard people had worked on the show. Woody himself had been brought back time and again to try to make it work. In the finish, I even tried once again to salvage at least some of the material in another show entirely, one we were planning to do on political satire. Unfortunately Woody was by then so outraged by what he was being told was our reluctance to show his work that he refused to make any more cuts. I had had no direct contact with him, which made it the more difficult.'

In historical perspective, who knows? The incident of the

169

PBS film-that-wasn't may turn out to have been of value, nonetheless.

Professor Day now runs a class in film and television at his university. He says: 'I show a private copy of the film (somebody gave it to me when our attorney on the case resigned) to my students every year, as a sort of bonus. To that extent it has proved educational.'

He also explains to them, citing the case as an object lesson, that political forces *can* control showbusiness, and do, when an election is pending. 'The paradox in Woody Allen's case,' he says, 'is that it involved a law where the regulations are intended to be fair to all candidates – that of allowing them each equal time. On this occasion it could have worked *against* Nixon.'

If, for instance, the programme had diminished the president's chances of re-election, by satirising him and his administration, would it, asks Professor Day, have been necessary under the rules of fairplay to run a similar send-up, or lampoon, of his opponents?

'The law (in the USA) also requires the media to give ten days warning to any subject it intends to attack,' Day adds. 'That's to allow time for defence measures. But in Woody's case there are two obvious items which could not have been exposed without counter-measures, and probably injunctions, to stop the show going on.

'One of these was when Woody, as Wallinger, says at one of Pat Dixon's dinner parties where she might be supposed to be offering Wallinger certain favours: "I don't go for that sort of thing." The implication was too obvious.

'The other was when, in the programme, the *New York Times* is described as a "homosexual newspaper". Apart from its bad taste, this was obviously highly libellous and damaging to every member of the paper's staff.'

The professor's students don't always get the point, though. 'They tend to ask me "what's all the fuss about?"' Day says. 'They admire Woody and claim him as their own, since he went to school across the street from our college in Brooklyn. And there's a line in the show – about tapping

170

"Dixon's phone" – which seems to them prophetic, in view of the Watergate mess which followed.'

Woody himself confessed to the programme having been in bad taste. His anger at the censorship was understandable, if misplaced. Had the show been funnier, perhaps it would have been possible to ignore the strict letter of the law. As it was, anything less than the action taken was bound to bring disastrous results. And public broadcasting in the United States – alone in receiving no support from commercial advertisers – has little power to support life as it is.

After Jim Day had ordered cancellation, Woody's show was replaced by a travelogue dragged out of the station's morgue: *Come to Florida before it's too late.* He might almost have chosen the title himself. His frustrated dislike of Richard Nixon had to stay bottled up until events took their course. And the portrayal of Harvey Wallinger (whose mother had been 'a mistress of Mussolini') will never be more than an item of historical interest. Disappointing, but Woody is not one to feast on failure.

As he told Dick Cavett during a televised interview (from the same station – Channel 13, New York) in September 1979, 'It was a silly little film . . . But there was a big to-do made over it at the time. I mean, they thought it was in bad taste . . . They would put it on if I edited certain remarks out of it. And, of course, by that time they had painted me into a corner . . . So what could I do? . . . I wouldn't give an inch and they wouldn't give an inch. And so finally they just dropped it. No great loss to anybody as it turned out . . . I think if you were to see it now you'd think, you know, amusing at best . . . But I got tired of it. Also, I guess, Public Broadcasting was funded by Washington and they got real sensitive.'

Cavett had reminded Woody of the time he, working then for Jack Paar, booked his friend onto the show, only to see him get involved in another censorship row. Woody's script contained an item about an island where the inhabitants thought food more seductive than sex. It upset some latent streak of puritanism in Paar, who wanted it cut out.

'But when they went to do the piece,' Cavett told Woody, who had almost forgotten the incident, 'they couldn't find anything to censor. So they took one word out . . . God!'

However, by the time of the interview, Woody was apparently more preoccupied by the need he felt to write serious work than by censorship. He had completed *Annie Hall* and had plans for *Interiors*. To Cavett – one of the few he talks openly to in public – he confessed: 'I was very frightened all the time that *Annie Hall* wasn't funny . . . I just had to make it on faith . . . and that's a very hard thing to do. Fortunately I got a lot of support from people around me, they kept telling me "don't worry, you don't have to be hilarious all the time" . . . But it's very hard for someone like myself, I think – any comedian – who's relied their whole life on response for laughter, to be willing to take chances like that. It's much more frightening than you'd think it would be.'

Yet he does take chances, and some – like his later film *Stardust Memories* – falter if not fail. In California in the early spring of 1981 Charles Joffe told his New Yorker friend Audrey Della Russo that criticisms of Woody's *Stardust* had 'totally baffled him: they just don't understand what he is trying to say.' In Joffe's home on the coast the Oscar he won as producer (for Jack Rollins and Charles H. Joffe Productions) of *Annie Hall* is now used, derisively, as a hat-stand. 'So that nobody can see where he's hidden it,' says Audrey.

She has known Charley Joffe long enough to know that his dedication to Woody is no light thing. 'I was with him at the *Bitter End* to see Woody give one of his first-ever performances. I didn't get it at all. Small, quiet and insignificant. To me, Woody was nothing. But Charley didn't see him that way; and he's not only a nice man, he's a very skilful and most conscientious manager.'

As Jack Rollins says, Woody will never hit the jackpot with everyone. Funny-bones differ. Woody seems funny only to those who find him so – whether or not (and for the most part it's not) they can explain why it is. When he turns his serious face to them, they feel cheated. Rollins insists that this is nobody's decision but Woody's. And that every-thing Woody does is, in a certain sense, comedy.

'There's a belief,' he says, 'that he is now having to decide between comedy and making serious pictures. I don't think that's the situation at all. He always has worked in and through comedy, except maybe to leave it to do some work he wants to do now and again, like *Interiors*.'

Rollins continues emphatically: 'No, he is going to stay in comedy, because that is what he does. But not everybody sees comedy the same way. What is funny to one is not to another. So, how Woody develops in future depends on his own choice, and his own way of expressing his personal view of life, which is entirely based on comedy for him. Ultimately, he always makes his own decisions.'

But what if it is not as simple as that? Empty seats close cinemas, as the Rank Organisation's decision in June 1981 to kill off a sixth of their 127 halls in the United Kingdom showed all too graphically. Woody's fans are restless. They don't all follow him into his more cerebral reaches. Paul Hoagland for one expresses anxiety about *Stardust* and the future. As this twenty-two-year-old Columbia student, reading Fiction Writing for a Masters Degree says: 'I liked Woody's movies when he was still unselfconscious. I liked them all, the old ones. Later, he got to parodying himself which, to me, hampered him as an artist. *Interiors* really disappointed me. It showed that he wasn't content with humour, he had to make us sad as well. And in *Stardust Memories* I'd say he is trying to *lead* his audience. So for me the movie fails because it is too forced, too obvious. What Fellini failed to do in $8\frac{1}{2}$ Woody is now attempting, and it doesn't work.'

Hoagland is typical of the central hardcore of Woody's keenest and most appreciative fans. He must, if he's to retain the golden image which still underwrites any film he cares to make – to the tune of millions of dollars – either bring them with him to the higher reaches of whatever slope of Parnassus he believes his further ascent must take, or change direction. The latter course would not seem to be on the cards.

'Money is of very little interest to him,' says Jack Rollins. 'What matters is being able to do the movies he likes, unhampered by interference and people bothering him. The closer he can come to that paradise, the more important it is to him.'

And this enviable goal, whatever fans like Paul Hoagland may say, remains almost miraculously within his grasp. His move towards serious pictures is a progression which can be charted with some accuracy and no lack of success, perhaps partly because, as Rollins points out, 'Extraordinarily, his pictures seem better each time you see them – so they keep getting shown.' Whether or not he consciously plans this, it does happen. And has, all through his fourteen-film career.

Five years ago, Woody declared that nothing he ever does is conscious. 'I never set out to do anything consciously,' he said, 'and sometimes I'm amazed at what gets a laugh.' In *Annie*, Woody explained, 'there's a little kid who says "I used to be a heroin addict. Now I'm a methadone addict." That always got such a laugh that you never heard the little girl he's talking to say "I'm into leather." And another big surprise to me which I didn't think at all funny was when I sneezed and the cocaine went all over the place.'

Since anyone with a normal sense of appreciation of the bizarre would be expected to react to the humour of the latter situation in the film – when a seemingly innocent (or *nebbish*?) Woody is handed a snuffbox of highly expensive white powder to take a minute sniff, only to sneeze and blow its contents to total loss – it has to be assumed that Woody sees comedy as a serious matter. It is even probable, in that case, that the reverse is also true: that serious drama, for him, can be funny.

Certainly, the path has led him away from the parody, the satire and the *slapschtik* into more subtle uses of his exquisitely distorted vision. In the early and middle Seventies he moved from the neurotic humour of *Sex* to a more sustained parody of science-fiction in *Sleeper* (1973) and from there, almost without pause, to a tongue-in-cheek mockery of sombre Russian drama, *Love and Death*. It was a long way from *Tiger Lily* but still not far enough.

To the magazine *Esquire* he attempted an explanation. 'The standard ploys of the professional funny man,' he said, 'are jokes about anguish and dread. Finality, morality, human suffering, anxiety.'

To intelligent Woody-watchers, this may have made sense. Max Liebman, who saw each of his films in turn, is still surprised that his silent, unsuccessful writer could have developed so far and so fast. 'I saw that he was beginning to philosophise,' Liebman acknowledges. 'His talent was in being intellectually funny, and that explained things to me. I saw he was on a different plane from comedy. He was no longer in what I'd call the commercial segment of the comedy world.'

Liebman witnessed the deeper, more serious side of Woody emerging in the role he played – unusually for him – in somebody else's film, *The Front;* the disappointing but well-intentioned story of Senator McCarthy's blacklist of writers.

'Then comes the time when he is almost stepping over the line,' Liebman explains. 'He wants to be the serious actor-writer. So he makes first *Annie Hall* then *Manhattan* and, somewhere in between, *Interiors,* where he shows a touch of Federico Fellini and Ingmar Bergman.

'Now he becomes what he is: a serious writer, using comedy only as a tool.'

To Max Liebman, this places Woody in an altogether different category. 'I think of him as the young intellectual,' he says, 'expressing the problems he meets and has to overcome in order to survive. Who to compare him with? Chaplin? Yes, Chaplin tried it with *Monsieur Verdoux,* and *Great Dictator* and *King of New York.* But I think Woody wants to be even more serious than Chaplin. I have to put Woody Allen in the category not of an entertainer but of an artist.'

And in Max Liebman's book, artists are not commercial. As he expresses it, 'When you're more interested in your work than in making money you may be "significant", but at a cost. Woody has taken, in my opinion, a step forward artistically and two steps back commercially, in order to retain his balance.'

The American novelist and critic Donald Newlove (*The Drunks; Those Drinking Days*) sees Woody's artistic life as only beginning. 'He's still in his first stage of being,' Newlove says. 'As an artist he's trying to break out. He hasn't yet reached his second flowering.'

Discussing Woody's controversial *Interiors*, Newlove agrees with Liebman that it was 'too imitative of Bergman's *The Silence*.' He explains: 'This is Kierkegaard trembling in the fear of God. Those tremendous waves in the beach scenes are a violent religious statement. They suggest an uncommunicable, speechless God. Woody Allen, like Bergman, is obsessed with death.'

The author equates all Woody's work with 'difficulties' in his private life. 'They spring from the man himself,' he says. 'They are personal shortcomings he tries to overcome. For instance, in *Love and Death* he's going to die. In *Sex* it's being born. He's moving towards the free soul, as Kafka did in *The Trial*, which put us all on trial. This sort of Jewish culture, of the Talmudic legal mind, is embedded in Woody Allen.'

Newlove argues that Woody has still to resolve a creative dilemma in himself, but may well do so. 'He's not happy with success,' he explains. 'The second stage of life can only be achieved by a complete equation of the ego, and Allen is possibly playing against the ego – the worm, the power, the super-ego, the drive. That's what he leaves out of his movies, this creative drive. He portrays himself as less than the full man capable of making these very sophisticated works, because he knows he has not yet reached where he's going. I'm sure he has sentimental feelings of pleasure from his accomplishments, but you can't rest on those. You have to deflate yourself and get right down into the Sahara of the soul. Then you can start again with something fresh and right that's really great. Only by bringing a new flowering can you avoid repeating yourself.'

Chaplin took ten years to find a sequel – a second flowering – to *City Lights*. Woody Allen, says Newlove, must search long and hard for his 'next stage of being' if he is to find fulfilment as an artist. Otherwise (and there are millions who want him to do no more than this) he can only stay where he is, making even those who don't know what he is trying to say, laugh.

Does he know this? To Britain's veteran film reporter Barry Norman, on BBC television late in 1980, Woody gave a strong indication that, if he does, it isn't going to make the slightest difference.

'I never feel any obligation to be funny,' he said. 'It astonishes me what a lot of intellectualising goes on over my films. They're just films. Yet they treat me like a genius at times, at other times like a criminal. Because I've produced "bad art"!'

But to writer Mel Karman whose unusually revealing interview with Woody Allen had appeared in a serious American film magazine three years earlier, Woody put it somewhat differently.

'You know, all the films I've done – *The Front* included – are personal failures. None of them leaves me with a good feeling, I mean. When I've finished them I don't want to see them again.'

Earlier, he had tried to explain to Karman *why* he made films. 'I'm just doing it to amuse myself and the half dozen people in my life that mean something to me. I never set out to do anything consciously. And I don't feel responsibility to any group in any way.'

Woody's personal taste, he admitted, was for 'the work of serious film makers and serious dramatists.' When he went to the movies he liked to see something by Bergman 'because I enjoy it more. It's more interesting, more meaningful.' Nevertheless, he was not ready to apply this to his work. Two films planned for late 1981 were both believed to be humorous subjects: 'Much like the old Woody,' one of them was described.

Earlier that year, 1981, Woody's third play, *Floating Light Bulb* opened to disappointingly lukewarm notices at New York's Vivian Beaumont Theatre. If anything, it exposed the fact that playwright Woody is a long way behind film scriptwriter Woody in development. His portrayal of an adolescent kid growing up in the Carnarsie section of Brooklyn, shy, nervous and helplessly driven by his mother to attempt the impossible (by performing half-practised magic tricks before a visiting showman) is plainly drawn from tormenting memories of his own youth. But the bitter humour of the situation is all but totally lost.

Describing it as 'an odd mixture of Neil Simon and Anton Chekhov', New York critic Clive Barnes wrote of the play in the *New York Post*: 'Tragedy is comedy seen from the inside . . . Allen's movies are characterised by a grievous sense of human comedy. One would have hoped that something of this would have penetrated through in *Floating Light Bulb*. But it simply doesn't.'

Woody had confessed to Barry Norman: 'Comedy is easier for me. To be serious, I often make a fool of myself. I am a whiner, a complainer.' And to Karman he had similarly admitted to a vision of depressing bitterness, often revealing itself as wryly humorous: 'Yeah, I'm real sour,' he said. 'And I'm a pessimistic person. A moderate depressive. And I don't have a healthy attitude toward things. Consequently it infuses my work, for better or worse.'

With despairing frankness, Woody Allen then summed up his personal and private dilemma, the flaw in his creative crystal which has audiences laughing uncontrollably at actions and attitudes he finds perfectly and seriously ordinary: 'I don't know why I am,' he told Mel Karman, 'I just am.'

Just being what he is has taken him to Olympian heights. Even Clive Barnes, whose critical pen can cut like a ripsaw, tempered his disillusionment over *Light Bulb* with the prayer that he would not 'frighten him (Woody) out of the theatre'. To Barnes, as he wrote, Woody Allen 'is one of the most sensible sensibilities in our time'. He is also, in middle-age, looking back on phenomenal success in all three fields he has given himself seriously to: films, theatre and literature. The question is: how seriously can he take himself and still make us laugh?

Regulah genius

It's not as if he doesn't recognise the problem. 'One day I think I'm going to wake up and find people have found me out, if they haven't already,' he said recently. 'I'm at the stage where I've got to be good, and perhaps I'll not be able to do it.' From an artist of Woody's manifold talents who has been accused, as he says, of 'having a sophomoric, shallow, narcissistic obsession with my own personality,' such candid insecurity is exceptional, if not unique. He really does doubt his capacity for maintaining the popularity he has enjoyed since that day in February 1964 when Charles Feldman offered him work on the film he so hates to be reminded of.

To intimates like Cavett he may joke: 'I'm moving towards total acceptance by the masses, but working to stop it'. In fact, as Jack Rollins knows only too well and Woody is far too intelligent not to recognise, he is caught in the nutcracker situation which has had demonic effects on so many creative and popular artists: the pressures of mass expectation.

'The next ten years?' Rollins says. 'Oh boy! I have a racehorse and that's like asking me if it's going to win its next race! I don't know. I *think* he'll keep developing, whatever that means. Because he always has. He wants to keep going, sure. That's all he wants.'

Rollins shakes his head. 'In a way,' he concludes, 'he's quite a simple person. But in other ways he's unusually complicated. Who knows what direction he'll go in?'

Maybe nobody, as Rollins implies. But there is around Woody in his forty-sixth year a small, tried corps of friends

179

and fellow workers who would make a substantial bet that it will not lead to bankruptcy, either of cash or creative talent.

Melvin Bourne is one of these. As production designer on *Annie Hall, Interiors, Manhattan* and *Stardust Memories* and now working on Woody's current productions, he has not the slightest doubt about Woody's capacity to go on to greater and ever more splendid heights.

'People don't realise how visual he is,' Bourne says. 'He sees it all clearly, knows exactly what he wants, and his working habits are impeccable – which may seem surprising in view of his casual manners and appearance.'

The man who has had in his time to face unexpected changes, such as occur in all feature film productions but can be swifter and more telling than most in Woody's case, is nevertheless unshakeable in his devotion to Woody Allen, director. Mel Bourne will not say a word against the man he regards as a genius in having brought in so many successful films. 'Woody,' he says, 'is totally prepared, always. He comes in and does his work, quietly and without fuss. He doesn't say much. And he's not much fun on the set; no laughs. With him, it's totally business while we're working. But he's a terrific guy. There's nobody better.'

Bourne and Gordon Willis, Woody's award-winning (*The Godfather* and many more) lighting-cameraman cinematographer, get as close as anyone to him in the course of their work. They are frequently forced into proximity by exterior locations and cramped quarters. Woody, wherever and whenever possible, shoots his films in and around New York. Willis says that the ideal would be 'to shoot in his own apartment on Fifth Avenue' where Woody maintains an opulently comfortable, surprisingly bourgeois lifestyle.

Having a completely free hand, he does the next best thing. Picking old and often derelict houses in unfashionable parts of Manhattan in which to endure the long grind of film-making. He hand-picks everyone who works with him. Yet there is no personal contact.

180

'We never see each other off the set,' Gordon Willis says. 'We're not close at all, on a personal level. I have my family and I like to get away to my home in upstate New York. Woody loves the city and hates to leave it.' Mel Bourne confirms this. 'I have no personal contact with him at all, really. Working even as closely as we do, we don't socialise. None of the unit does.'

Woody sees nothing strange in relating to different people on altogether separate levels. His continued use of Willis and Bourne shows how he feels about their work, but as social friends he admits only those few rare companions he has drawn into an enclave of his own making. The perceptive Mel Karman, having pointed out to Woody that he had this tremendous loyalty to Diane and Tony Roberts and all his friends, asked him point blank: 'How does one become your friend?'

Woody's reply is among the most revealing attempts at public confession he has ever made – though doubtless rehearsed many times on his analysts' (the latest, reportedly, a woman) couches: 'It's *very* tough. I'm real guarded.'

In qualifying this he seems to contradict both Willis and Bourne: 'I guess,' he told Karman, 'you work on a project with somebody and gradually you find that you like them. I don't know *why* you like them.'

If only it was that simple, as Mel Bourne says, it would be fairly easy to follow the direction of Woody's curious friend-selection antennae. 'But he doesn't even allow people in to see the dailies ('rushes' of the previous day's shooting, much prized as indications of a film's progress),' Bourne points out. 'Except for Gordon and me and the editor, and of course the producer whenever he wants to see them, nobody is allowed in.'

According to the talented New York photographer David McGough, who specialises in taking pictures of Woody, the chauffeur who drives Woody's Rolls is never invited to talk to his employer. McGough, who once had his camera kicked by Woody as he tried to snap him under the brim of a pulled-down, broad, felt hat from pavement level, says the chauffeur told him in 1980 that he and his master 'haven't exchanged more than a few words over the three years he's driven him.' McGough says: 'Woody tells him where to go and when he wants to be picked up. That's all he ever says, or has said.'

Readers of New York's gossip-columns imagine Elaine Kaufman to be a close friend of Woody's, but she denies it. Elaine's crowded, excitingly small restaurant up on New York's Second Avenue is one of Woody's favourite haunts. He and Mia Farrow were there night after night during their courtship. David McGough and other *paparazzi*-style photographers were usually in attendance. But although the dark, comfortably plump, Russian-born proprietress is on close enough terms with Woody to tell him what she thinks of his films, she still sees their relationship as being no more than distant.

'I don't sit down and eat with him,' she says, 'And I only talk to him once in a while. I keep a table for him –' She points to the far end of the long, narrow darkly-lit room with the crowded bar stretching half way along its length '– that one there, at the very back. It seats about eight or ten people. And Woody always comes in, when he does, with a group of close friends. The same ones every time. If they don't get here by ten thirty, then I know he's not coming.'

Elaine, like Mel Bourne and Gordon Willis, enjoys a close working relationship with Woody. Like them too, it stops short of anything personal. 'But we talk, maybe, about his work,' she admits. 'For instance I had this point of view about one of his films, and I told it to him. He just smiled and said he didn't see it that way. So I told him "Well, that's the way it comes out." And he laughed.'

The film Elaine criticised was *Stardust Memories*. Elaine's objection was that Woody had failed to realise in it the fictitiousness and falsity of Hollywood glamour. 'I understood what he was getting at,' she says. 'The agony and toil, both emotionally and socially, of being a creative person like him. But I believe it's really the same for everybody. The cab driver he meets in the film says "I'm just a cab driver", but as I told Woody there's no difference between him and a Hollywood star, only that people in America think there is.'

So from time to time Elaine is permitted the privilege of telling her best customer what she thinks. Very few others can do so, without bruising whatever relationship they have. Elaine is valuable to Woody. She protects him, by, as she says, 'just once in a while stopping somebody being a nuisance to him.' She also understands and favours his very specialised, cautious likes and dislikes. 'He drinks tea, not coffee,' she explains. 'His taste in food is simple. He likes only health-giving food and good wine. He particularly likes a good claret, a Bordeaux; but he'll drink a Burgundy occasionally. He likes fish and is very fond of pasta dishes. The point is, he's very selective.'

Elaine sees Woody as a highly sensitive, artistic individual whom she respects for his work and his long-standing use of her restaurant. Yet she thinks he is misunderstood. 'He's not indifferent to what people think,' she says. 'Even the way he dresses is not as casual as people believe. He dresses to be comfortable. But with care.'

She agrees that he is probably over-sensitive – even allergic – to many things he feels are hostile to him. But about food he finds disagreeable she says, 'It's hard to tell what he really won't eat. He'll take a chance with his work, but with food and drink he doesn't ever try anything new, it seems to me. In Paris they say he ate the same dish, filet of sole, every night. Well, I wouldn't be at all surprised.'

You see Woody differently if, like David McGough and New York's other master *paparazzi*, Ron Gallela, you spend long weary – often wet and freezing (or stifling) – hours on pavements and in parked cars waiting to take a picture of the shy superstar. As McGough says: 'He's a joke to most photographers, but he's not funny to me. He's more like a little mouse running down the hole. It's not funny at all.'

Only when McGough finally met Woody did he discover a likeable side to him. Woody telephoned one night, asking if – to repay McGough for the accident to his camera – the photographer would like to take pictures at rehearsals for his new play. David McGough went along, met Woody, and found him both more introverted and nicer than he'd imagined. He explains:

'So then he let me come up to Mia (Farrows)'s house and I wondered how I could get them to loosen up. I mean, I'd been after them for so long. When I finally do get them together, I asked myself, how are they going to react?'

Convinced that both Woody and Mia would close up like frigid clams, he prepared a gift for them. As he says: 'I really believed they were married, though no announcement had been made. So I took along a small present, and a card saying "Congratulations! May you be very happy, always."'

Woody and Mia were appreciative, says McGough – until Woody read the message. Jack Rollins describes the gift, and Woody's reaction to it (a shouted 'We're married? Of course we are!') as anybody's normal reaction to such a 'stupid thing to have done'. He says: 'Woody just said the opposite. Of course he did. He and Mia weren't married at the time, but that stupid photographer annoyed him to the point where he would have said anything.'

David McGough may be stupid to Rollins, but he knows his business and is prepared to stake-out Woody, and other hard-to-get stars, for pictures their fans are craving to see. He recalls the night Woody kicked his camera, leading up to the wedding gift episode:

'This particular night we'd had to wait three hours in the pouring rain. I was with Mr Gallela on the corner of 74th Street, right by Woody's apartment at 930 Fifth Avenue. When he did come, he was alone.

'What happens is that the guards always tell him if we're there, or not. So he came out knowing what to expect, and he clamped this floppy hat right down low over his head. As he's almost a foot shorter than me – I'm six foot three – I dropped right down low to try to shoot under the brim. And what happened was he kicked me. He didn't have much choice, I'm bound to say, because I was right in his way. Well, let's say he *could* have avoided me, but he didn't. And I won't say it was all his fault because maybe I should not have been right where I was.'

Since this is exactly the sort of incident Woody portrays in *Stardust Memories*, cynics credit him with deliberately provoking such relentless coverage. It is a fact that the media is forced to adopt its worst keyhole tactics in his case. Woody, like it or loathe it, is hot copy. To McGough, who moved on to him from rock stars like Mick Jagger, he is 'a superstar, but not in the same class as Robert Redford or Barbra Streisand. I'd say a low superstar. He's special, and I don't know why.' One reason could be that Woody Allen, like Greta Garbo and Albert Schweitzer before him, has inadvertently backed into more limelight than he would ever have had shone on him if he'd done what most celebrities do – laid himself wide open to it.

That's not to say it is a deliberate pose. Those who work the long, nail-biting weeks of a film's shooting with Woody see an altogether different side of him. Randy Badger was a location manager on *Stardust* who respects Allen as 'among the best directors around today', a view shared almost unanimously in film circles. Nevertheless Randy found Woody's intense perfectionism hard to take.

'I didn't like working with him,' he says now. 'Sure, he's immensely creative and talented, and he tries very, very hard. But he's completely professional, just does his job then leaves the set. There's no personal contact with him, no warmth at all.'

If Randy finds this unpleasant, other perfectionists like Gordon Willis accept it as a refreshing change from directors who cover ineptitude and uncertainty with chatty bonhomie. Since Woody hired Willis to photograph *Annie Hall* the two have worked closely together on every one of Woody's pictures. Willis believes the greatest virtue of their relationship is a shared refusal to accept the second rate. And a near identical sense of humour.

'We're individuals,' he says, 'but we make a good marriage. Because basically we like the same things, and feel our way along the same tracks. Even if sometimes we fall off!'

It helps that Willis appreciates Woody's sense of comedy. 'He has excellent taste,' the cinematographer explains. 'He knows just how far to go. He can make an intimate scene inoffensive. And we do see things very much the same way.'

A major factor, because as Willis says: 'In comedy especially, it isn't always easy to share another person's view. Woody has a very well-developed way of visualising things for himself. I mean, I'm not his optic sense. But we do harmonise.'

Others find it much harder to do so. A woman who worked as one of the senior assistants among Woody's editorial crew on *Annie Hall* and *Interiors* complains about his lack of any sort of relationship with the unit. 'It was a pretty disconsolate group to work with,' she says. 'We all had to eat with Woody – that was a royal command. But he kept a pretty dull table. Nobody was allowed to smoke. And none of us could leave until he was ready to go – which was the moment he finished eating. Woody's fantastic at meals, he bolts his food then can't sit around a second afterwards. Unless he happens to get involved in long, technical discussions. These can go on for hours.'

To Mel Bourne and Woody's most loyal, inner group of film-makers, all directors must be allowed certain foibles. Woody's seem irrelevant, in view of his perfect coordination with his henchmen in bringing to successful completion such masterpieces as *Annie Hall* and *Interiors*. Bourne is not alone in preferring to work with Woody than almost any other director. But neither is he wholly uncritical.

'Woody,' he admits, 'does kind of take it for granted you're going to be there to work for him whenever he wants you. That isn't always easy when other films come up.'

Actors relate to Woody in two ways. Some blossom under his curiously remote way of directing them. Others resent his apparent stand-offishness. Bourne says: 'I had many friends on *Interiors* – Jerry Page and Maureen Stapleton, notably – who loved him. They're crazy about the way he works, which is very individual. I tell you, a whole lot of players really adore him. But, I admit, there are also those who can't stand him.'

The same split occurs often between Woody's senior

technicians and talented creative artists.

'We had a first-class costume designer, Albert Wolsky, on *Manhattan*,' Bourne says. 'He couldn't bear to work with Woody. He felt he was useless, because there was no personal contact and that was something he absolutely had to have.'

And Mel Bourne admits: 'Woody can seem to be heartless. He's very direct always. And extremely self-centred. But that's because he knows what he wants and won't take any part of anything less.'

A designer has to work closely, almost intimately, with his director. In Bourne's case he finds this stimulating, enriching – and occasionally upsetting. 'We have our disagreements,' he says wryly. 'He can make me very cross with him at times, when changes are costly and time is running out. At the beginning of *Stardust*, I thought we'd never get it right. He'd just sit around and say "I don't think this is going to work." My spirits would drop down to zero. In the end, that sort of thing is bound to get you down.'

And Mel, no masochist, looks back with a shudder on some of their worst moments.

'I'd say *Interiors* was the trial of the age to me. That was the *worst*. He'd change entire sets suddenly – because he'd last-minute decided he just didn't like them. Yet . . .' Bourne scratches his head perplexedly, 'in the end it turned out exactly right. The way he'd seen it.'

He adds, in admiration and certain wonder: 'And when the chips are down, he'll come round a little. He's not a dictator or a hard-assed driver of a unit. He's a human being, definitely. Without the least interest in anyone's personal problems, though, when you're working together. No compassion. You've got to know that if you're going to work with him.

Mel Bourne continues thoughtfully: 'I don't say he's easy, not at all. And I'm not one who worships him. I just believe that the man comes as close as anyone can get, in my book, to being a complete master of what he is doing – which has never been an easy thing: that is, to make a successful moving picture.

'To do it, he'll be utterly ruthless very often, and with his own material as much as anyone else's. It's the end result he cares about. Only that.'

This faith, despite Woody's coldness to even the closest of his fellow technicians, stems directly from an appreciation of his professional skills. It has to, since in Bourne's experience Woody is impatient with anything, even personal injury or sickness, which stands in his way.

'I happened to break my ankle ski-ing, last February (1981),' Mel Bourne recalls. 'It was a bad break, in three places, and I had the entire leg set in plaster, right up to my crotch. When we left his apartment and I had to get into Woody's car, it took a lot of wriggling around and lifting in of the thing. This didn't please him at all.

'Woody finally turned to me and asked: "How long are you going to have to keep that thing on?" I told him: "It might be weeks. Depends how long it takes the bone to knit." "Well, I'm fed up with it already," he said, and I must say he looked it. All I could think of to reply was "I'll tell my doctor".'

This mild sarcasm was lost on Woody. He appears not to notice the animus occasioned by his remoteness. Bourne says, 'He's very secretive. We go up to his apartment with him a lot while we're working, especially on the preparation of a film, like now. (Note: this was in April 1981 when Woody was working on two scripts for shooting later that year). Yet we get to know almost nothing about him.'

The designer reflects. 'I don't think anyone but Tony Roberts and Diane, and maybe one or two others, get close to him.' He laughs. 'At least that means you don't ever get into real spats. Because the relationship has to be exclusively professional from first to last.'

As to Woody's attitude to the often gruelling and exhausting process of making a moving picture – an attitude he has described as painfully necessary but seldom pleasant – Mel Bourne has learnt to take Woody's initial enthusiasm with a large dollop of salt. 'He'll say at the start, "We'll have a lot of fun on this one, even if we fall flat on our faces." That was what he told me when we were planning

Stardust. He'd said much the same thing on the earlier movies. It just never works out that way.'

Why not? 'Because Woody knows every inch what he wants. And he gets it, in spite of every opposition. Sometimes he makes changes which knock you sideways, but it's always clear in *his* mind what he does them for. The worst are those he is capable of making on the morning of shooting. He can come in, see a whole set ready to work in, then decide he doesn't want it. So out it goes.'

But as Mel Bourne sums up: 'He is one hundred per cent professional. Generous with faults in others, provided they're not stupid or deliberate. He'll ask for the impossible, but when told it will take too long he'll listen and be reasonable. In fact he *is* very reasonable, compared to a lot of other directors. I'd say with Woody you're working under very good conditions, comparatively.'

Always, there is the qualification. Woody's persistent claim to be just a nice little guy, sweet and harmless – to Barry Norman, a 'whiner, a complainer' – sounds far less convincing when those privileged to work with him describe their experiences. For one thing he is, as Rollins underlines heavily, essentially uncomplaining. The notion he purveys of ineptitude, and of suffering a failure to enjoy life which he refers to as 'anhedonia' (his discovery of the word and its curiously fitting meaning is in itself highly revealing); his notorious need for psycho-analysis (though somehow never relieved by it of his much publicised weaknesses); his total insecurity at parties, with strangers, and whenever his work is praised or shown for the first time; all of these argue fundamentally against the picture of Woody at work and in social contact painted by those close to him.

He knows it, too. Talking to Gene Siskel of the *Chicago Tribune* one Sunday last summer, 1981, he admitted that work was the governing discipline of a life in which spinelessness marks his every other move. Parties, he can't face entering; cities, despite his well-known love of New York, are becoming anathema; getting a woman to join him in bed can present impossible difficulties if it means 'changing the subject'; and an irrepressible inability to 'gracefully interact with people' are more than symptoms of Woody's personal malaise: they could be a raiment he wears, subconsciously ('nothing I do is conscious') to attract maximum attention.

Don't listen to me, he seems to be saying at the top of his lungs. I'm a loner, always have been – provided I can eat out in crowded restaurants every night and live in one of the world's most densely populated cities. When you prick me, look – blood! And all this is Woody's individual fantasy-*verité*, a dream, an illusion, created to guarantee him the notice of an outside world he cannot, must not, be contaminated by.

The boy who wanted to be a lavatory attendant at Midwood, who thought magic the silk-ladder of his dreams of escape, and who has tumbled headlong into middle-age without apparently having grown up, is locked inside the man-machine of Woody Allen, one hundred per cent professional, compassionless, ruthless and stonily reserved. A talented performer to family and friends – and even to those who would rather take their holidays on the moon than make a film or play with him.

Add it all together and what have you? In the phrase of any Jew to describe a more successful brother, with only the thinnest crust of satirical admiration and envy – a regular (or, as they'd satirise it in Woody's America: 'regulah') genius. How far that takes him from Newlove's 'second flowering' may be the question he would find most hard to answer.

To Siskel he confided: 'I do have an agenda for myself. I'd like to make a series of great films. I would like to try to overreach myself and challenge the great film-makers.' How long that will take nobody would like to try and guess; or how long before he accepts, as the majority of his contemporaries and a growing world public accept, that he is fully entitled to a high place in their ranks already.

'I think he'll go on making changes, a lot of changes,' says Melvin Bourne. 'The style of his work, the searching, will constantly be there. But the content will change, unlike Doc (Neal) Simon, who is always the same. Woody never wants to repeat anything. He'll be using new ideas, new thoughts and he'll not only work enormously hard to make them come alive, he'll expect us to. Woody doesn't care if you kill yourself, because he does the same with himself.'

On reflection, Mel Bourne also sees how only Woody can be the arbiter of his own decisions and directions. 'I evaluate it like this. Some of his pictures I like. But often what I think of the script when we start has turned out the opposite in the finish. When I read *Stardust* for instance, I thought it was going to be the greatest movie ever. It wasn't. But that was an editing failure as much as anything else. I'd thought *Interiors* was going to be difficult, yet it turned out well. *Manhattan* I thought inconsequential when I first read it, but it was a great film. And *Annie Hall* was a gem. That was the only one I knew from the start as a winner.'

So Mel Bourne and Gordon Willis and Jack Rollins and everyone else who shares the golden limelight cast by Woody's genius are banking on the same unexpected, often indiscernible, flair carrying him on to continuing and growing triumph. 'Do I feel happy about the two films Woody is going to direct, from his original screenplays, later this year?' Bourne asks rhetorically. 'Yes, I do. They'll run together, you see, one following the other, and from what I've seen and know, they'll be fine. I say that because I have absolute faith in him. I can tell you, too, that they're both comedies.' (Woody has since confirmed that of the earlier of the two). 'I'd say the first is a little closer to popular comedy, while the second is what I'd call interesting. It's going to be a tough one to do in some ways, but in another way it could be very simple. We'll just have to wait and see.'

As we all will. Forecasting Woody Allen's future has never been easy. A few weeks before he won his Academy Award for *Annie Hall* Woody gave a touching, wholly unpublicised demonstration of his total unpredictability. It also underscored a generosity and sweetness which is glimpsed and loved by those, and only those, who lay claim to being his friends.

Woody, the man who seems 'cold' to many of those he works with, who won't talk to people on the street, sat down and wrote in his own hand a short letter to a lady in Brookfield, Connecticut.

Isabelle Bates had written to Woody first. Her grand nephew was depressed. The song 'Short People' was popular, and the boy was being teased constantly at school because he was well below average height. 'I had the thought,' Mrs Bates explains, 'that many successful people are short. If I wrote to them and told them of little (see, I even did it!) Steve's plight, they might give him a few words of encouragement.'

Woody Allen was one of those she chose to write to. And he was among the first to reply. His letter reads: 'Dear Mrs Bates: Tell your nephew don't forget about that little ol' ant, who moved that great big rubber tree plant, (with a little help). 'PS. Tell him to write me again when he's 21, if he's still the same height. Woody.'

As Isabelle Bates says, winning an Academy Award may have been important to Woody Allen at that moment. But he still found time to win a special place in the heart of one undersized youngster.

Perhaps, knowing that, we should take him more seriously than we do.

It's time, it's time

The question, of course, is – as a New York paper headlined its interview with Woody recently – 'How now, Woody Allen?' *Where is he headed*? And is it plausible to explain his motivation as a mere quirk, a compound of inborn shyness and ethnic wit? It may be. At the very least, it offers something we can all nod our heads to, even Woody himself.

If one did not know that he is not joking when describing his reluctance to face the world, equally in fame or failure, it might be reasonable to assume a pose on his part. But this is a man who is afraid to enter a crowded room; who does not know exactly *why* these fears afflict him, or what it is that burns his bridges into ordinary social life. He admits it. In a rare burst of confession he put it to Gene Siskel that, 'When I was 19 . . . I won a Sylvania Award . . . and there was a dinner given . . . a big honour for me. And I went up to the door and I couldn't go in and I never did go in. I went home, and I felt so relieved when I got home. And I've repeated that problem or syndrome or symptom many times.'

All he can do is give it names: 'anhedonia' – a word unlisted in most English dictionaries, but said (by Woody) to describe an inability to enjoy pleasure, is one he woefully revels in; another is 'entering phobia', which comes closer to plain speech. Anyone doubting that it is a real condition, as chronic as arthritis, should be with Woody during the hours of self-preparation necessary to his appearance at a social gathering. 'I've tried to be the first one . . . If it's called for eight o'clock, I'll show up at 7.55,' he admitted to Siskel. 'If only I could materialise in there . . .' The thought of vanishing into a disembodied presence, free to roam at will without interference or the need to communicate, appeals to him enormously. Subconsciously, he was seeking something of its sort when he brought home his first magic tricks to practise in the comforting stealth of his childhood bedroom in Brooklyn. In all his relationships, in marriage and even in the grip of passionate affection such as he undoubtedly feels for those closest to him on occasion, there is the same tendency to ethereal remoteness. Some part of Woody Allen belongs elsewhere.

Yet he makes the real world laugh. More than the clown with heavy heart and painted smile, Woody is a classic case: the sufferer who makes fun of his pain, and of ancient grief. In us all is at least a small part of his 'little loser'. Recognition of this in his work lends his appeal a universal charisma. Only because he cannot see this *from the outside*, Woody Allen refutes any suggestion of genius, but of course that is what he has and what he is. The first essential of art is that it should communicate a vision never before expressed on the subject. Only through the distorted prism of genius can Man obtain this, and irrespective of his or her own understanding of its transcending viewpoint. So one thing at least is clear about Woody; his own opinion about himself is not the most reliable.

His school's present headmaster explains that genius is something 'we know nothing about', and this strikes at the very heart of Woody's dilemma and the failure of both his schools and family well-wishers. He was clever enough, and in many ways dutiful and generous enough, to want to conform to the pattern he felt shackled by. What it cost him to go against his parents' wishes is unlikely to be more than a distant, bitter memory now, softened by all that he has done for them since. But it was agonising at the time, of that there can be no doubt.

The point is that it had to be. The Woody Allens of life are, more than most, driven. They can buck the tide, but at a cost which may destroy not only them but all who come in contact with them, and who assume the subconscious role of their jailer. For the eccentric, the artist, and the genius in all walks of life, society has only one meaning: it is the audience, the public, the world outside his or her tiny and vulnerable shell. Its weight is terrifying, its ways anathema. But it is as necessary to reach out to it as it is to breathe air.

Woody's failures in marriage correspond exactly to this pattern. He reached out too far, seeking the warmth he was given to expect from fellow human beings. But without realising that his is a unique path, one that can only be walked in solitude or with a companion who is so undemanding as to be almost unnatural. Perhaps now he has come to understand this.

And knowledge of his foibles, as of his capabilities, came equally slowly. At school it was mainly boredom that drove him to scribble those acutely satirical, pungent and sometimes mercilessly destructive observations on the human condition, those gags which earned him much more than the pocket-money he gained from them initially. If he had had to exist without them, the same ennui may well have driven him to excel. School work was never too hard for him, it was merely uninteresting. And the curriculum of school life, the warp and weft of educational fabric, failed to draw him towards it. In revolt, he silently escaped into whatever alternative offered itself. His success with gags convinced him that there *was* a world outside Midwood and Flatbush, a sphere where the dull warnings of school, synagogue and home had no place. And where a man's natural gifts might earn him the wherewithal of subsistence.

If he needed support for this heresy, university and college life supplied it in full measure. The acid test of his independence was in their halls. They, even more than Midwood, underrated his worth, for the very good reason that he gave them as little of himself as possible. Parting from the glades of academe was mutually and urgently necessary.

So the disappointment he felt when Max Liebman's laboratory of writers opened its doors, only to give him a temporary and unsatisfying resting place for his talents, was keen. It was also shared, since the woman he had married as a refuge from the stultifying and damaging pressures of Hollywood was at his side. It was to be many years before the flaw in that match came to the surface, years when the grind and dedication of a full-time professional role at Tamiment summer camp slowly, relentlessly split them apart. Though it arose painfully from this shattered union, the persona of Woody Allen had no choice: like the sun over the Tamiment lake, it simply had to rise and take possession.

The mistake he had made was one common to artists. He carried unwanted baggage, a wife whose qualities were not in doubt. Harlene was a fine and intelligent companion; but one who could not move with him into the narrow arena of his creative role. What she failed to accept, even if her instinct suggested it, was that *no* woman could have joined in his development at that time. The chrysalis had burst open; Woody had discovered the magic of flight.

With Louise, his second attempt at marriage, the undertaking was underwritten by their joint awareness of its frailty. Both had their careers, separate yet overlapping. Both knew that they could pace out the road together for only as long as it led in the same direction. Once that ceased to be, the parting would be without recrimination. After the trauma of Harlene's understandable bitterness and pain over his wholly unconscious misuse of their marriage as a subject for his most pointed parody, it was the only basis on which he could conceivably have consented to any subsequent marriage.

With its inevitable end, and the further maturing of his shared yet limited capacity for relationships with women, in the months shared with Diane Keaton, Woody showed that he had come of age. The artist and the man were at last one. He was no longer striving to behave as parents, relatives and teachers would have him believe he should behave. He was being himself. So the work to which he gave increasing priority grew in individuality and style entirely according to his own whims and wishes. Plays, films, writings and music ceased to be work carried out as a means to obtain the necessities and luxuries of life: they were life itself.

The conventional world and its rule-book faded into a background belonging to others, not to him. The need for a hand-picked group of close and loyal friends and lovers, exclusive even to those he worked most closely with, became paramount. The natural world – the country – was an alien land, disturbing and in some ways belittling his creative appetite. It was the city, his own city of New York (though not its affluent, conservative suburbs and outlying districts), which held and cradled him in its arms. Here, far more than in Paris or Rome or London, he could close the shell around him and settle, like some aquatic mollusc, against the safety and seclusion of its rock-face. Here, he was in tune.

The work was, notwithstanding, a persistent tight-rope. Each separate creation had to be engaged in with the care of a delicate, expectant mother. Unable to accept repetition or compromise, he had to risk every venture afresh, telling himself that public acclaim, opinion even, must not be heeded. Yet knowing that if he failed to achieve a positive result, at least with the faithful, the fall would be long and painful.

A consolation lay in his versatility. What he found unsuitable for the wider canvas of cinema he could fashion into a play. Intangible, surrealist notions flowed onto paper as pieces more often than not accepted with delight by Roger Angell and his colleagues of the prestigious *New Yorker*. The few still-births – notably those, like his Public Broadcasting television skit on Nixon and Kissinger, suppressed by censorship – irked but did not dismay. There was always the warm knowledge that Hollywood coffers were open to him. Mammon might lack insight and understanding, but it knew where to place the tokens of its faith.

And always there was the kindly, shrewd and able support of Jack Rollins and Charley Joffe, never wavering for a moment in their convictions about him. While increasingly he came to doubt the validity of outside opinion, knowing it to be coloured by deference, their sounding board was a much needed and practical prop.

As with his writing, new techniques, styles and modes of expression had to be learned. Film production is not noted for its guardian angels, and the sheer weight of money committed to even the least indulgent picture can terrify those executives in it. He, with each successive production, had to recognise a deceptively concealed reality: that his standing with the filmworld's financial backers was only as firm as the box office returns from his last picture.

And of course the budgets grew. It would take a C. Northcote Parkinson to categorise the swings and counter-swings of Hollywood economics. Woody's maverick genius lacked all the known standards of success – the star casts, vastly expensive exploitation and 'hype' of each element, and the false belief that money lavished on exotic sets, huge crowd scenes and pampered players will attract public support. He simply made pictures, and in the way he knew – the only way he knew – he could do so. Because whatever form it took the sprite guiding his 'optic sense', as Gordon Willis describes it, seemed blinded by anything else.

We see him today not on a new and decisive brink, as Newlove and others suggest, but facing exactly the same crisis of selection as he has come up against since *Tiger Lily*. The same, one could say, since opting for gag-writing in place of more conventional forms of education. Before him, as before any truly creative artist, lies the unexplored unknown.

Which path to take, is the besetting question. And the equipment he must take on the journey – safely tried comedy or the stronger though perhaps less practical props of serious drama.

For Woody Allen is not a stationary orb. He is in motion in a universe sparkling with similarly mobile planets and stars, suns and moons. Among the living and the dead of this cosmic sphere he must find an instinctive course or lose his brilliance. At present he stands, if the stellar analogy is to be pursued, on the cusp. The heavens about him are bright with promise, yet filled with danger of collision, eclipse and extinction. What we are seeing in our aesthetic night sky is a beloved star pausing in its soaring path. Before falling? Before rising to greater heights? We must, as Woody Allen must, wait and see.

Index

204